Designing Scalable Systems

The Art of Growth: Scalable Solutions for Tomorrow

Huzaifa Asif - Asim Hafeez

Designing Scalable Systems

Copyright © 2024 by Huzaifa Asif & Asim Hafeez

www.huzaifa.io | hello@huzaifa.io

ISBN: 9798875582813 (Paperback)

ISBN: 9798875584855 (Hardcover)

First Edition

Designing Scalable Systems

"Designing Scalable Systems" is a book that guides you through the important steps of making scalable systems that can grow and change easily. In today's fast-moving tech world, businesses and developers need to know how to build systems that can handle high traffic and large volumes of data without problems. This book covers everything you need to know about how to plan and build these kinds of data-intensive systems.

The Essence of Scalable System Design

Scalable system design is an art that balances technical proficiency with foresight and adaptability. It's about building systems that can handle growth – not just in terms of user numbers or data volume but also in complexity and functionality. The need for scalability stems from the dynamic nature of technology and user expectations. Systems that fail to scale effectively can lead to performance bottlenecks, increased costs, security vulnerabilities, and ultimately, a diminished user experience and lost business opportunities.

Navigating Through the Chapters

Chapter 1: API Protocols

We begin our journey with an exploration of API protocols, a critical component in system scalability and efficiency. The right choice of API protocol – be it SOAP, REST, GraphQL, or others – can significantly influence a system's performance and its ability to scale.

Chapter 2: Software Architectures

Next, we turn our attention to software architectures. This chapter emphasizes the importance of selecting an architecture that aligns with the project's scale and complexity, considering factors like team size and skill set.

Chapter 3: System Design Process

The system design process is then examined, highlighting the importance of clear planning and defined boundaries. This chapter guides you through each phase of system design, ensuring that the final product aligns with business goals and is prepared for future scaling.

Chapter 4: Databases and Data Management

Databases and data management are the backbones of any scalable system. This chapter focuses on choosing the right database and managing data effectively, considering factors like data volume, velocity, and variety.

Chapter 5: Cloud Solutions and Infrastructure

The discussion then shifts to cloud solutions and infrastructure, exploring the modern cloud landscape, containerization, orchestration, and automation. This chapter provides insights into leveraging cloud technologies for scalability and efficiency.

Chapter 6: Scaling

The chapter on scaling addresses the challenges and strategies of scaling systems. It covers horizontal and vertical scaling, database optimization, caching strategies, and the selection of the right architectural framework.

Chapter 7: Monitoring

Monitoring is crucial for identifying and addressing performance issues in scalable systems. This chapter covers network monitoring, real-time analytics, and various monitoring strategies to ensure system health and performance.

Chapter 8: Big Data & Analytics

Big Data and Analytics are explored next, emphasizing their role in understanding and utilizing large datasets to drive business decisions and enhance user experience.

Chapter 9: System Security

System security is paramount in scalable system design. This chapter explores security violations, program threats, and comprehensive security measures to protect against a wide range of threats.

Chapter 10: Cost Optimisation

Finally, the book concludes with a chapter on cost optimization, a critical aspect of maintaining the financial viability of scalable systems. It discusses strategies to manage and reduce costs without compromising on quality.

The Importance of a Holistic Approach

This book is designed to provide a holistic understanding of scalable system design. Each chapter is interconnected, emphasizing that a successful system is not just about excelling in one area but achieving a harmonious balance across all aspects. The failure to adhere to best practices in any of these areas can lead to significant issues, ranging from poor performance and security breaches to financial losses and reduced market competitiveness.

For Whom This Book Is Written

"Designing Scalable Systems" is written for a diverse audience – from software architects and system designers to developers and project managers. Whether you are building a new system from the ground up or scaling an existing one, this book offers valuable insights and practical advice.

As you embark on this journey through the pages of "Designing Scalable Systems," you will gain not just theoretical knowledge but practical skills and strategies to design systems that are robust, efficient, and ready to grow. This book is your guide to navigating the complexities of scalable system design, ensuring that you are well-equipped to meet the challenges of today's fast-paced technological landscape.

Table of Contents

CHAPTER 1

API PROTOCOLS

CHAPTER 1

API PROTOCOLS

I have observed numerous systems evolve, expand, and, unfortunately, sometimes falter. A recurring theme in these experiences is the pivotal role that API protocols play in the scalability and efficiency of a system. This observation has not only piqued my curiosity but has also driven me to explore deeper into understanding the nuances of various API protocols.

Why devote an entire chapter to API Protocols in a book about designing scalable solutions? The answer lies in the countless instances where I've seen systems struggle or fail not due to the lack of innovative ideas or robust infrastructure but because of the inappropriate application of API protocols. Consider a messaging system bottlenecked by RESTful calls when the real-time bidirectional communication offered by WebSockets would have been a more fitting choice. Or picture a complex inter-service communication system, entangled in GraphQL queries, where the simplicity and efficiency of gRPC or message queues could have streamlined processes.

It's evident that choosing the right API protocol is not just a technical decision; it's a strategic one that can significantly impact the scalability and performance of a system. This chapter aims to shed light on the different types of API protocols - SOAP, REST, GraphQL, gRPC, Web Hooks, and Web Sockets. We will explore each protocol in detail, discussing its advantages, limitations, and ideal use cases.

By understanding these protocols in depth, you'll be equipped to make informed decisions about which to use and when. It's not uncommon for a robust system to employ multiple protocols, each catering to specific features and scenarios within the system. Our goal is to provide you with the knowledge to discern which protocol aligns best with each aspect of your system's architecture, ensuring efficiency, scalability, and resilience.

As we embark on this journey through the world of API protocols, remember that the key to a scalable and efficient system lies in the foundation of its communication pathways. Let's begin by discussing the intricacies of these protocols and their impact on the world of scalable system design.

1.1. Introduction

API protocols are sets of rules and conventions that controls the communication and interaction between different software systems or components through an Application Programming Interface (API). These protocols set the rules for how data and requests should be prepared, sent, and received, making sure that different software can understand and cooperate with each other well. Common API protocols include:

- SOAP
- REST
- GraphQL
- GRPC
- Web Hooks

- Web Sockets

1.2. SOAP (Simple Object Access Protocol)

SOAP stands for Simple Object Access Protocol. It is a lightweight messaging protocol that is based on XML and allows the various parts of an application, which are located in different locations or systems, to exchange information and communicate with each other.

1.2.1. Understanding SOAP: Functionality and Operation

It works by taking organized data and putting it into XML format, then sending it using different network methods like HTTP and SMTP. It follows specific rules for how messages should be formatted and shared, making it possible for different parts of separate programs to easily share information.

This guarantees dependable communication that can work on various systems and locations without any problems.

SOAP (Simple Object Access Protocol)

1.2.2. Benefits of Using SOAP

- It makes sure that when information is sent, it follows a strict set of rules so that both the sender and receiver can understand it easily. This is particularly useful when it's crucial to keep the data correct and reliable.

- SOAP supports ACID Transactions.

- It includes built-in capabilities to implement various security measures, such as WS-Security, that facilitate message-level encryption, authentication, and authorization.

- It includes various reliability features like message confirmation and retry mechanisms, which can be employed to guarantee the dependable delivery of SOAP messages.

- It offers a consistent method for dealing with errors using fault elements within the message. This simplifies the process of identifying and resolving problems.

- It supports both stateful and stateless operations.

1.2.3. Challenges with SOAP

- It is not natively supported in web browsers, which can be a disadvantage when building web-based applications that require client-side communication.

- Its API is not cacheable.

- It messages often contain a lot of unnecessary information, which can make them less efficient when sent over a network.

- The developer community doesn't frequently use it these days.

1.2.4. Effective Use Cases for SOAP

- **Enterprise Systems:** It is often used in enterprise applications, such as ERP and CRM systems. These applications typically require high security, reliability, and extensibility, all of which SOAP provides.

- **Healthcare systems**: It's strong security features make it an ideal option for securely exchanging medical records and patient information, where maintaining data privacy and integrity is of utmost importance.

- **Finance Sector:** It is used to facilitate secure and reliable transactions. Banks and financial institutions employ SOAP to ensure the integrity, confidentiality, and ACID compliance of sensitive financial data, which is crucial for maintaining the consistency and reliability of their financial operations.

1.3. REST (Representational State Transfer)

REST stands for Representational State Transfer. It is a modern and flexible architectural style for designing networked applications. Unlike SOAP, REST doesn't prescribe a strict messaging protocol but rather emphasizes a set of principles for building scalable and efficient web services.

1.3.1. Understanding REST: Functionality and Operation

It uses standard HTTP methods to communicate with resources via URLs. Clients send requests, and servers respond with data, typically in JSON or XML. This stateless, URL-based approach simplifies communication and enhances scalability for building distributed systems.

REST (Representational State Transfer)

1.3.2. Benefits of Using REST

- It is simple to understand and use. It relies on standard HTTP methods like GET, POST, PUT, and DELETE, making it easy to work with.

- It supports caching, which can improve performance and reduce server load by allowing clients to cache responses.

- RESTful APIs tend to be more efficient than SOAP because they typically use lightweight data formats like JSON or XML, allowing for faster data transfer over the network.

- REST APIs are scalable. They can be used to build high-performance APIs that can handle a large number of requests.

- SOAP messages are heavy in content and consume greater bandwidth, REST should be used where network bandwidth is the constraint.

1.3.3. Challenges with REST

- The REST APIs are not as secure as SOAP APIs. They do not have built-in security features, such as WS-Security.

- They do not have built-in reliability features, such as message confirmation and retry mechanisms. That's why they are not as reliable as SOAP APIs.

- SOAP APIs can be more performant than REST APIs. This is because REST APIs typically use HTTP methods, which are not as efficient as SOAP's XML messaging format.

1.3.4. Effective Use Cases for REST

- In **Social Media**, RESTful APIs are provided by platforms to allow developers to interact with user profiles, create posts, fetch content feeds, and seamlessly integrate social sharing capabilities into external applications.

- **IoT Apps:** They are also used to build IoT applications. This is because REST APIs are scalable and can be used to connect a large number of devices.

- **Cloud Computing:** REST supports cloud computing in controlling how URLs are decoded during client-server communication.

1.4. GraphQL - A Query Language for APIs

GraphQL is simple Query language for APIs and a runtime for fulfilling those queries with your existing data. GraphQL was developed by Facebook in 2012 and released publicly in 2015. It has since become one of the most popular API technologies, due to its flexibility, efficiency, and ease of use.

1.4.1. Understanding GraphQL: Functionality and Operation

It functions by enabling clients to precisely define the data they want from the server, eliminating data over-retrieval or under-retrieval. This approach optimizes client-server interactions, making GraphQL a favored option for contemporary API development, prized for its adaptability and efficiency.

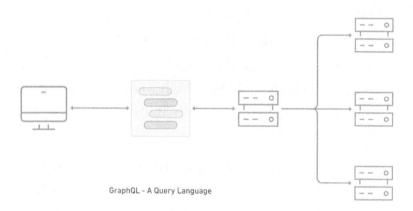

GraphQL - A Query Language

1.4.2. Benefits of Using GraphQL

- It has a simple and intuitive query language, making it easy for developers to learn and use.

- GraphQL follows a client-driven architecture that enables clients to specify the precise data they require.

- GraphQL technology typically uses a single endpoint for all API operations, simplifying the API surface and reducing the need for multiple endpoints. This makes it easier to maintain and understand.

- It allows clients to precisely request the data they need, preventing the unnecessary retrieval of excessive data and ensuring efficient and optimized network utilization.

- It can also support real-time data updates through subscriptions, allowing clients to receive updates when relevant data changes, making it suitable for applications like chat or live feeds.

1.4.3. Challenges with GraphQL

- GraphQL can lead to complex queries, and it's essential to manage query complexity to prevent performance issues or security vulnerabilities.

- Caching in GraphQL can be challenging due to its dynamic nature. Unlike fixed data structures in REST, caching GraphQL responses require thoughtful strategies to maintain cache efficiency.

- Inadequately optimized GraphQL queries can lead to performance issues, such as the infamous N+1 problem. Ensuring efficient query patterns and data fetching is vital to maintain optimal response times and server performance.

1.4.4. Effective Use Cases for GraphQL

- **Real-time Data Applications**: Good choice for real-time data applications, such as chat apps and social media apps. This is because GraphQL allows clients to subscribe to specific data fields and receive updates whenever the data changes.

- **Data Aggregation:** it is handy when you need to gather information from various places, like combining data from different databases or APIs into a single format that clients can easily use.

- **Content Management Systems** often utilize GraphQL to provide a convenient and efficient way for content creators and developers to access and modify information with flexibility.

1.5. gRPC (gRPC Remote Procedure Calls)

gRPC is developed by Google, is an open-source framework for remote procedure calls (RPC). It offers a language-agnostic and platform-independent approach to building fast and distributed applications.

gRPC is built upon HTTP/2 and Protocol Buffers, ensuring it is both efficient and lightweight. It allows different parts of a program to communicate with each other, connecting to applications spread across multiple locations, and calling their own functions or methods as needed.

API Protocols

gRPC (gRPC Remote Procedure Calls)

gRPC's success can be attributed to its adoption of HTTP/2 over HTTP/1.1 and its use of protocol buffers as a replacement for XML and JSON.

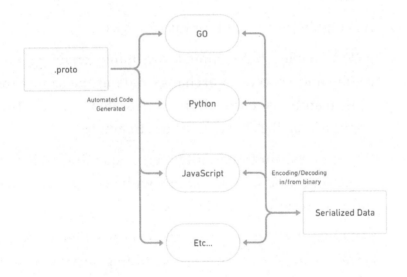

DATA SERILISATION WITH PROTOCOL BUFFERS

1.5.1. Understanding gRPC: Functionality and Operation

It operates by enabling clients to send structured requests, typically in Protocol Buffers format, to servers through defined methods within a service. The server processes the request and responds with structured data, also commonly in Protocol Buffers format. This communication is facilitated by the efficient HTTP/2 protocol, allowing data to be transmitted bidirectionally between client and server. Protocol Buffers ensure efficient data encoding and decoding during this exchange.

1.5.2. Benefits of Using gRPC

- gRPC is faster than REST APIs that use JSON because it uses binary serialization and HTTP/2, which are more efficient.

- It is highly performant for microservices.

- gRPC enables bidirectional streaming, enabling both clients and servers to exchange data at the same time. This feature is particularly well-suited for real-time applications like chat and video streaming.

- It supports multiple languages, enabling seamless communication in applications with services written in different programming languages.

- gRPC is platform-agnostic, making it suitable for use across a range of platforms, including servers, mobile devices, and web browsers.

1.5.3. Challenges with gRPC

- gRPC can be more challenging to learn than REST, especially for developers unfamiliar with Protocol Buffers, due to its use of service definitions and ecosystem.

- As It uses HTTP/2, which may not work well with older systems or certain firewalls, making it less suitable for some environments.

- Compared to REST, gRPC is a newer technology with a less mature ecosystem, resulting in fewer available libraries and tools.

1.5.4. Effective Use Cases for gRPC

- For **Microservices**, gRPC is an excellent option. It's efficient, lightweight, and offers bidirectional streaming support.

- In **Polyglot Environments**, It serves as a universal communication protocol, facilitating interaction between services written in various programming languages.

- For **IoT Applications**, Its efficient and real-time data handling capabilities make it an ideal choice, enabling rapid and seamless communication between devices.

1.6. Web Sockets - Real-Time Communication

Web Sockets represent a communication protocol that facilitates simultaneous two-way communication over a single TCP connection. Unlike traditional communication methods, where one party must wait for the other to finish before responding, WebSockets enable both the client and server to send and receive messages in real-time.

Although WebSockets are layered on top of HTTP/1.1, they employ a distinct framing protocol that enhances efficiency when transmitting data. Consequently, WebSockets are particularly well-suited for real-time applications like chat systems, video streaming platforms, and multiplayer games.

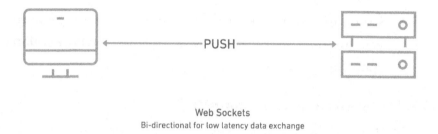

Web Sockets
Bi-directional for low latency data exchange

1.6.1. Understanding Web Sockets: Functionality and Operation

WebSockets enable real-time, bidirectional communication between a client and a server. The process begins with a handshake, where the client requests an upgrade from HTTP to WebSocket protocol, and the server acknowledges. Once established, this persistent connection allows both parties to exchange data freely and simultaneously, unlike the request-response model of HTTP. The connection remains open for ongoing interaction, with both sides capable of sending data at any time. The connection is closed only when either the client or server sends a closing handshake, ensuring an orderly termination of the session.

1.6.2. Benefits of Using Web Sockets

- This protocol reduces latency by keeping a persistent connection open between the client and server. This guarantees swift transmission of data, making it a valuable choice for applications that rely on rapid updates.

- It offer scalability and have the capacity to handle a high volume of concurrent connections effectively.

- Web Socket is widely supported by modern web browsers and is adaptable for use with a variety of programming languages and frameworks, making it a versatile solution for developing web applications.

- It operates on an event-driven model, delivering data as soon as it's accessible, eliminating the necessity for polling. This feature is advantageous in situations where rapid client responses to events are essential.

- Web Sockets can serve as a replacement for long-term polling.

1.6.3. Challenges with Web Sockets

- Implementing WebSockets can be more intricate compared to other communication protocols like HTTP.

- WebSocket connections are stateful, necessitating server resources to keep connections open, which may pose scalability difficulties when managing numerous concurrent clients.

- Distributing WebSocket connections among multiple server instances for load balancing can be more challenging than handling traditional HTTP requests. It may necessitate specialized load balancing solutions or the management of sticky sessions.

1.6.4. Effective Use Cases for Web Sockets

- **Gaming:** In the realm of online multiplayer games, WebSocket technology is frequently employed to facilitate real-time, low-latency communication between players and the game server.

- **Financial Trading Platforms:** WebSocket proves itself as a fitting choice for financial applications demanding swift data updates, including stock market tickers and trading platforms.

- **Real-Time Chat:** WebSockets excel in real-time applications due to their support for full-duplex communication and low-latency performance.

1.7. Webhooks - Event-Driven Data Delivery

Webhooks are a method of real-time communication between web applications and services. They differ from WebSockets, which maintain an ongoing connection, by using HTTP callbacks to alert one application about events or data modifications occurring in another.

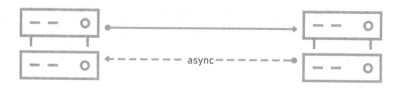

Web Hooks
Asynchronous for event-driven applications

1.7.1. Understanding Webhooks: Functionality and Operation

Webhooks are a method for achieving event-driven data delivery, allowing applications to receive real-time

16

notifications of specific events. When an event occurs in a source application, it triggers a Web Hook, which sends an HTTP request (typically a POST) to a specified URL - the target application's endpoint. This mechanism enables the target application to react immediately to changes or updates, without the need for polling the source. Web Hooks are widely used for integrating diverse systems, enabling them to communicate and update each other automatically. The simplicity and efficiency of Web Hooks make them ideal for scenarios where timely data synchronization or event notification is crucial.

1.7.2. Benefits of Using Webhooks

- It facilitates asynchronous communication by enabling the sender to inform the receiver of events without the need for an immediate response, making them valuable in situations where real-time, bidirectional communication is not required.

- They ensure secure communication through the utilization of HTTP requests and SSL encryption, establishing a dependable choice for transmitting sensitive data.

- Webhooks enable a decentralized architecture where numerous senders can independently notify multiple receivers, making it well-suited for situations where diverse systems must communicate without depending on a central hub.

- It makes it easier to connect different systems because you don't have to keep asking if there's something new, it tells you right away when there is, saving time and resources.

- Unlike WebSockets, which need to keep connections open all the time, webhooks don't require this. This means that the systems receiving information don't have to work as hard, making things easier on the server and using fewer resources.

1.7.3. Challenges with Webhooks

- Webhooks depend on network connections and server availability, so they may not always deliver data reliably if there are network problems or the server is down.

- WebSockets enable two-way communication, whereas webhooks are one-way, allowing data to move only from the sender to the receiver.

- If your system is not online when a webhook is sent, there are only a few attempts to deliver it before stopping. Be sure to have an alternative plan to get the data if your system is down for an extended period.

1.7.4. Effective Use Cases for Webhooks

- **CI/CD Platform:** Webhooks automate code builds upon developer repository changes, ensuring efficient and consistent development workflows.

- **Database Updates:** It serves as a real-time method for updating databases, particularly beneficial for applications requiring constant data synchronization.

- **Logging:** It is used for logging events and activities in real-time, enabling applications to maintain comprehensive and up-to-date log records.

CHAPTER 2

Software Architectures

CHAPTER 2:

SOFTWARE ARCHITECTURES

We're going to talk about something that's super important but often overlooked: software architecture. Think of it like planning a big trip. Before you start, you need a good map to guide you, showing you the best routes and what you can expect along the way. That's what software architecture does for building software.

Why is this chapter important? Well, in the world of building software, not all projects are the same. Some are like quick trips to your local store, while others are like long, adventurous journeys. The 'map' or architecture you choose should match your journey. If you pick the wrong one, you might end up lost, or it'll take way longer to get where you're going. That's why understanding different types of software architectures is super important.

But here's the thing: choosing the right architecture isn't just about the technical stuff. It's also about your team. How big is your team? What are they good at? What does your project really need? Sometimes, teams pick a fancy architecture like microservices because it's popular, but it ends up making things harder, especially if the team is small or the project isn't that complex.

So, in this chapter, we're going to help you understand these different architectures and how to pick the right one for your project. It's all about making sure you have the right map for your journey, so you can get to your destination smoothly and successfully. Let's dive in and find the best path for your software project!

2.1. Introduction

Software architecture is like the master plan for building software. It's the big-picture design that shows how all the different parts of the software will work together to do what it's supposed to do. The significance of software architecture lies in its role as the foundational framework for the entire software development process. It profoundly influences the system's scalability, maintainability, performance, and other critical characteristics, shaping the system's quality and long-term viability.

We are going to discuss some of the architectures

1. Layered or N-tier Architecture

2. Microservices Architecture

3. Event-Driven Architecture

4. Web-Queue-Worker Architecture

5. Big Data Architecture

6. Service Oriented Architecture (SOA)

2.2. Layered or N-tier Architecture

Layered or N-tier architecture is a software architecture pattern where an application is divided into multiple layers or tiers, each responsible for a specific set of tasks. Typically, these layers include a presentation layer (UI), a business logic layer, and a data access layer. Communication between these layers is usually structured in a hierarchical manner, with each layer depending on the services provided by the layer beneath it.

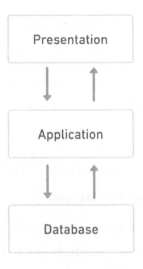

N Tier Architecture

2.2.1. Optimal Scenarios for Layered Architecture

Layered architecture is suitable for a wide range of applications, especially those where separation of concerns and modularity are essential. It's commonly used in web applications, enterprise software, and systems where scalability and maintainability are important.

2.2.2. Key Benefits of Adopting Layered Architecture

- You can secure each of the three tiers separately using different methods.

- N-tier architecture is very friendly for development, as different teams may work on each tier. This way, you can be sure the design and presentation professionals work on the presentation tier and the database experts work on the data tier.

- If you want to introduce a new feature, you can add it to the appropriate tier without affecting the other tiers.

- Compatibility with heterogeneous environments, offering flexibility across both Windows and Linux ecosystems.

2.2.3. Practical Scenarios: Layered Architecture Use Cases

Web-Based E-commerce Platform:

- **Presentation Layer**: Manages the user interface, displays products, and handles user interactions.

- **Business Logic Layer:** Controls shopping cart functionality, order processing, and discounts.

- **Data Access Layer:** Connects to a database for product information retrieval and storage.

Social Media Platform:

- **Presentation Layer:** Displays user profiles, posts, and notifications.

- **Business Logic Layer:** Manages friend requests, post sharing, and privacy settings.

- **Data Access Layer:** Connects to a database for user data storage and retrieval.

2.2.4. Case Study Insights: Layered Architecture in Practice

PayPal:

- **Architecture Overview:** PayPal, a leading online payment platform, utilizes a layered architecture to manage financial transactions securely.

- **Layers:** Presentation (web and mobile interfaces), Business Logic (transaction processing and fraud detection), Data Access (customer and transaction data).

- **Benefits:** Layered architecture ensures robustness, scalability, and compliance with stringent security standards.

Amazon Web Services (AWS):

- **Architecture Overview:** AWS, the leading cloud computing platform, employs a layered architecture to provide various cloud services.
- **Layers:** Presentation (web console and APIs), Business Logic (service orchestration and management), Data Access (data storage and retrieval).
- **Benefits:** The layered approach allows AWS to offer a wide range of scalable and modular services to millions of customers worldwide.

2.2.5. Navigating Challenges in Layered Architecture

- The risk of creating an intermediary layer primarily focused on CRUD operations for database management can introduce unnecessary delays without contributing meaningful functionality.

- The management of an Infrastructure as a Service (IaaS) application entails more effort compared to an application relying solely on managed services, adding complexity to the operational tasks.

- Monolithic design hinders the ability to deploy individual features independently, leading to a lack of flexibility in rolling out updates and improvements.

- Implementing robust network security measures can become a formidable task within a sprawling and intricate system, posing challenges in safeguarding data and communication channels effectively.

2.3. Microservices Architecture

Microservices architecture is an approach to software development where an application is divided into a collection of small, loosely coupled services, each responsible for a specific business capability. These services can be developed, deployed, and scaled independently, often communicating through APIs or lightweight protocols.

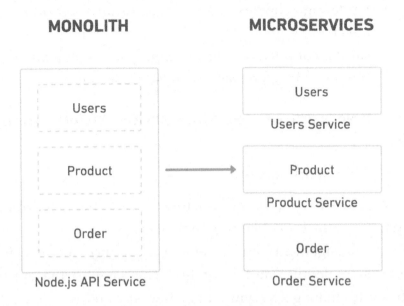

2.3.1. Optimal Scenarios for Microservices Architecture

Microservices architecture is well-suited for large and complex applications, especially those with rapidly changing requirements. It's commonly used in cloud-native applications, e-commerce platforms, and distributed systems.

2.3.2. Key Benefits of Adopting Microservices Architecture

- Services can scale independently, enabling the efficient allocation of resources by using orchestrators like Kubernetes or Service Fabric to pack more services onto a single host.

- Teams have the flexibility to choose the technology stack that suits their service, allowing for a mix of technologies as needed.

- Updating schemas is simplified in microservices as it affects only one service, whereas in a monolithic app, it can be complex due to multiple parts interacting with the same data, posing risks to schema changes.

2.3.3. Practical Scenarios: Microservices Architecture Use Cases

- **Ride-Sharing App**

In a ride-sharing app, microservices offer versatility. Separating functions like ride matching, payment processing, driver management, and user reviews into microservices provides scalability and flexibility. This enables the app to efficiently manage varying demand, streamline payments, onboard drivers, and enhance user experiences, all while adapting to evolving market needs.

- **Video Streaming Service**

Microservices in a video streaming platform enable efficient content recommendation, transcoding, authentication, and billing. This architecture ensures scalability, personalized content suggestions, seamless playback, and agile billing, enhancing the user experience and adaptability to industry changes.

- **Financial Services**

Microservices can be employed by financial institutions to manage tasks such as account management, transaction processing, fraud detection, and reporting. This approach boosts security and flexibility, enabling easier compliance with evolving regulations and market dynamics.

2.3.4. Case Study Insights: Microservices Architecture in Practice

- **Netflix**

Netflix is a prime example of a microservices architecture. In this setup, each service, such as user authentication, content recommendation, and streaming, operates as an independent microservice. This approach empowers Netflix to scale and update individual components without causing disruptions to the entire system.

- **Uber**

Uber utilizes a microservices architecture for its ride-hailing platform. Each microservice handles specific tasks like user management, ride matching, and pricing. This approach offers scalability, faster development, fault isolation, and technology flexibility.

2.3.5. Navigating Challenges in Microservices Architecture

- In a microservices application, there are more components in motion compared to an equivalent monolithic one. While each service is straightforward on its own, the overall system is more intricate.

- Ensuring efficient communication and data consistency between microservices can be complex.

- Coordinating the deployment of multiple services can be intricate.

- Extensive inter-service communication can lead to network congestion and delays. Long service dependency chains can worsen latency.

- Microservices are intricate distributed systems. It's essential to assess whether the team possesses the skills and expertise required for success.

2.4. Event-Driven Architecture

Event-driven architecture (EDA) is a pattern where components of a system communicate through events. Events represent meaningful occurrences within the system and can trigger reactions or updates in other components. EDA is often used to build real-time and responsive systems.

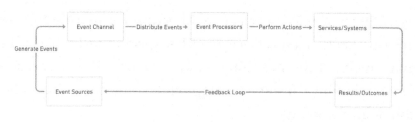

Event-Driven Architecture

2.4.1. Optimal Scenarios for Event-Driven Architecture

EDA is suitable for systems that require real-time data processing and responsiveness, such as financial trading platforms, IoT applications, and online gaming.

2.4.2. Key Benefits of Adopting Event-Driven Architecture

- Events can be processed concurrently, improving system throughput and reducing bottlenecks.

- Extremely scalable and widely distributed.

- Avoiding direct point-to-point integrations simplifies the process of incorporating new consumers into the system.

- Producers and consumers are decoupled.

2.4.3. Practical Scenarios: Event-Driven Architecture Use Cases

- **Real-time Stock Trading Platform**

A stock trading platform uses EDA to process and react to market events in real-time. When a significant price change occurs, events are generated and processed to update user portfolios and trigger buy/sell orders.

- **Healthcare Patient Monitoring**

In this use case, a healthcare institution adopts Event-Driven Architecture (EDA) for the continuous monitoring and care of patients. Vital signs are gathered from diverse monitoring devices and processed as events in real time. If significant changes are identified, healthcare providers are promptly alerted for timely intervention.

2.4.4. Case Study Insights: Event-Driven Architecture in Practice

- **Twitter: Real-time Notifications**

Twitter relies on EDA to deliver real-time notifications to its users. Events like tweets, mentions, and direct messages trigger instant notifications to keep users engaged and informed. EDA ensures that users receive timely updates on their activities.

- **NASA: Space Mission Monitoring**

NASA utilizes EDA in its space mission monitoring systems. Events from various spacecraft and instruments are continuously processed to monitor mission status, detect anomalies, and make real-time adjustments to ensure the success of space missions.

2.4.5. Navigating Challenges in Event-Driven Architecture

- Ensuring that events are delivered reliably and consistently can be challenging.

- Handling a large volume of events and their processing can strain the system.

- Debugging EDA systems can be complex due to the asynchronous nature of events.

- Guaranteed delivery. In some systems, especially in IoT scenarios, it's crucial to guarantee that events are delivered.

2.5. Web-Queue-Worker Architecture

Web-Queue-Worker architecture is a pattern where web requests are initially received by a web server, then queued, and later processed by worker processes or services. This architecture helps decouple request handling from resource-intensive tasks.

Software Architectures

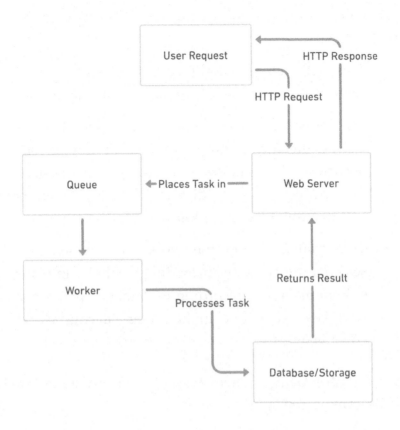

Web-Queue-Worker Architecture

2.5.1. Optimal Scenarios for Web-Queue-Worker Architecture

It's commonly used in applications that require background processing, such as job queues in web applications, batch processing systems, and email delivery services.

33

2.5.2. Key Benefits of Adopting Web-Queue-Worker Architecture

- This architecture is designed to be straightforward and easy to comprehend, making it accessible for developers to understand and work with.

- The architecture enforces a clear separation of concerns, ensuring that different parts of the system are responsible for distinct tasks, promoting maintainability and modularity.

- The front end and the worker components can be scaled independently, providing flexibility in managing system resources according to demand. This scalability is a key advantage in handling varying workloads effectively.

2.5.3. Practical Scenarios: Web-Queue-Worker Architecture Use Cases

- **E-commerce Order Processing**

In e-commerce platforms, this architecture can be used to manage order processing. Web servers receive customer orders, and enqueue them, and worker processes handle tasks like inventory management, order fulfillment, and payment processing.

- **Email Processing**

Email service providers can use this architecture to manage email processing. Web servers receive incoming emails, and enqueue them, and worker processes handle tasks such as spam filtering, routing, and message categorization.

- **Stock Trading Platform**

Financial platforms can adopt this architecture to process stock trading orders. Web servers accept trade requests, enqueue them, and worker processes execute trades, perform risk analysis, and update user portfolios.

2.5.4. Case Study Insights: Web-Queue-Worker Architecture in Practice

- **Twitter**

It uses a web-queue-worker architecture to handle its high volume of traffic. The web tier consists of load balancers and web servers that handle user requests and generate messages for the queue. The queue tier uses Amazon SQS to store and process the messages. The worker tier consists of worker processes that consume the messages from the queue and perform the requested tasks, such as posting tweets, processing notifications, and generating analytics.

- **Airbnb - Handling Listing Updates**

Airbnb, a popular vacation rental platform, uses a web-queue worker architecture to manage property listings. When hosts make updates to their property details, web servers enqueue these updates, and worker processes handle tasks such as data validation, search index updates, and notification to potential guests. This approach ensures consistency and responsiveness across their platform.

2.5.5. Navigating Challenges in Web-Queue-Worker Architecture

- Ensuring that workers can handle increasing workloads without bottlenecks.

- Properly managing queues and ensuring task prioritization can be complex.

- It can be difficult to monitor a web queue worker architecture system to ensure that it is performing as expected. This is because the different components of the system can interact with each other in complex ways.

- Handling worker failures and ensuring no data loss during processing.

2.6. Big Data Architecture

Big Data architecture refers to the design of systems that can collect, process, and analyze massive volumes of data. It often involves distributed storage, data processing frameworks, and specialized tools for analytics.

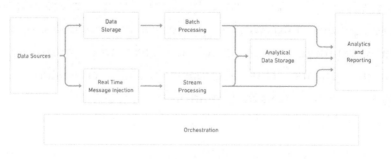

Big Data Architecture

2.6.1. Optimal Scenarios for Big Data Architecture

Big Data architecture is used in applications dealing with large datasets, such as social media analytics, recommendation engines, and scientific research.

2.6.2. Key Benefits of Adopting Big Data Architecture:

- The architecture can be easily scaled to handle large volumes of data by adding more web servers and worker processes.

- The components comprising Big Data architecture can be leveraged for IoT data processing and enterprise BI solutions as well, facilitating the creation of an integrated solution that spans multiple data workloads.

- Utilizes distributed computing and storage to optimize resource utilization.

2.6.3. Practical Scenarios: Big Data Architecture Use Cases

- **Smart Cities Traffic Management**

Big Data architecture can help manage traffic in smart cities. It collects and analyzes data from various sources, including traffic cameras, sensors, and mobile apps, to optimize traffic flow, reduce congestion, and enhance overall transportation efficiency.

- **Supply Chain Optimization**

Big Data helps optimize supply chain operations by tracking the movement of goods, analyzing supplier performance, and predicting supply disruptions. This ensures efficient logistics and reduced operational costs.

2.6.4. Case Study Insights: Big Data Architecture in Practice

- **Facebook's Personalized User Feeds**

Facebook employs Big Data architecture to meticulously analyze and personalize user feeds, enhancing the user experience. The platform adeptly gathers and processes extensive volumes of user interaction data, leveraging this information to curate and deliver tailored content to individual users.

- **Netflix - Content Recommendation**

Netflix employs a Big Data architecture to power its recommendation system. It collects and analyzes user data, including viewing history, preferences, and demographic information, to provide personalized content recommendations. This system has significantly contributed to the platform's success and user retention.

2.6.5. Navigating Challenges in Big Data Architecture

- Big Data architectures often involve integrating data from various sources, which can be complex and time-consuming.

- Handling increasing data volumes while maintaining performance is a challenge.

- Protecting sensitive data is crucial, especially in analytics.

- Achieving low-latency processing for real-time applications can be a significant challenge, especially when dealing with distributed data processing.

2.7. Service Oriented Architecture (SOA)

Service-Oriented Architecture (SOA) is an architectural approach where software components (services) are designed to be reusable and can be accessed over a network. These services are loosely coupled and can communicate through standardized protocols.

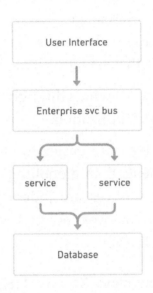

Service Oriented Architecture

2.7.1. Optimal Scenarios for Service Oriented Architecture

SOA is well-suited for large-scale enterprises, government systems, and organizations where integration of diverse systems and applications is critical.

2.7.2. Key Benefits of Adopting Service Oriented Architecture:

- This architecture can scale horizontally by adding more service instances, ensuring the system can handle increased workloads.

- SOA services can be implemented in different programming languages and run on different platforms. This makes it easier to integrate SOA applications with existing systems.

- It can lead to cost savings through code reuse and more efficient resource utilization.

- SOA applications are easier to change and adapt to new requirements than monolithic applications. This is because SOA services are independent of each other and can be updated or replaced without affecting the rest of the application.

2.7.3. Practical Scenarios: Service Oriented Architecture Use Cases

- **Government Agency**

A government agency has harnessed the power of Service-Oriented Architecture (SOA) to seamlessly integrate vital functions like tax collection, public records management, and healthcare data exchange. Through SOA, they've broken down data silos, improved cross-departmental collaboration, and enhanced efficiency, benefiting both internal operations and citizen services.

- **Content Management**

SOA transforms content management, seamlessly integrating web content, document management, and digital assets. It's like building with modular blocks for flexibility and scalability. This streamlines content creation and collaboration, delivering seamless online experiences across industries.

2.7.4. Case Study Insights: Service Oriented Architecture in Practice

- **Amazon's Service-Oriented Architecture**

Amazon's success as an e-commerce giant is partly attributed to its extensive use of SOA. They have built a robust ecosystem of services that handle various aspects of their business, from product catalog management to payment processing. This modular approach enables Amazon to continuously innovate and scale its operations while maintaining high availability and reliability.

- **United Airlines**

They utilize SOA to optimize their reservation system and enhance customer relationship management. This enables a seamless, personalized experience, streamlining bookings and improving customer support, elevating overall satisfaction and loyalty.

2.7.5. Navigating Challenges in Service Oriented Architecture

- It can be a complex architecture to design and implement. It is important to have a clear understanding of SOA principles and best practices before embarking on an SOA project.

- Ensuring backward compatibility when services are updated is a challenge.

- Securing the communication between services and managing access control is crucial.

- Ensuring data consistency across services can be challenging, especially in distributed systems.

- Applications that rely on SOA can pose management challenges due to their composition of numerous distinct services. It is crucial to implement a robust management solution to ensure visibility and control over all services within the SOA architecture.

CHAPTER 3

System Design Process

CHAPTER 3:

SYSTEM DESIGN PROCESS

In the world of software development, the system design process is a fundamental aspect, crucial for building strong, scalable, and efficient systems. This chapter explores the details of this process, highlighting its importance as we've seen many systems struggle with scalability issues caused by poor planning and vague processes. The path of system design is more than just following a set of steps; it involves creating a system that satisfies present requirements and can also smoothly adjust to future needs and changes.

A common issue in system design is the lack of clear boundaries. Without well-defined limits, engineers may inadvertently expand the system's scope, leading to a product that, while technically advanced, does not align with stakeholders' intentions. This misalignment can transform a well-intentioned feature addition into a complexity that skews the entire system's perspective. Similarly, inadequate planning of system flows, interactions between applications, and data modeling can lead to a distortion of business logic, resulting in a system that deviates from its intended purpose.

Therefore, this chapter is dedicated to guiding you through the entire system design process, ensuring that each phase is approached with thoroughness and foresight. We will cover:

1. **Requirement Gathering and Stakeholder Communication:** Understanding business objectives, identifying functional and non-functional

requirements, engaging stakeholders, and evaluating constraints.

2. **Defining System Boundaries and Scope:** Clarifying system components, interfaces, external dependencies, and responsibilities.

3. **High-Level Architecture Design:** Developing conceptual architecture, choosing styles and patterns, and defining component relationships.

4. **Creating Architecture Diagrams and System Flows:** Utilizing flowcharts, the C4 model, UML overviews, and ERDs for effective visualization.

5. **Detailed Component Design and Specification:** Refining interfaces, specifying behaviors, designing data models, and developing algorithms.

6. **Integration and Interface Design:** Defining integration points, designing API contracts, and ensuring data consistency.

7. **Security and Compliance Considerations:** Addressing security requirements, authentication, data privacy, and regulatory needs.

8. **Scalability, Performance, and Reliability Design:** Planning for scalability, optimizing performance, and designing for fault tolerance.

9. **Validation, Verification, and Testing:** Reviewing decisions, conducting verifications, and performing testing.

10. **Documentation and Knowledge Transfer:** Creating architectural documentation, communicating design decisions, and ensuring adaptability.

By understanding and following a structured system design process, we can create systems that are not only functionally sound but also scalable, maintainable, and aligned with business goals. This chapter aims to equip you with the knowledge and tools to navigate the complexities of system design, ensuring the end product is a testament to good planning and clear vision.

3.1. Requirement Gathering

3.1.1. Understanding Business Objectives

To understand the business goals better, we need to think about two important things.

- **Objective Alignment**

In this initial phase, it is important to engage proactively with top leadership and key stakeholders to gain a deep understanding of the organization's primary business objectives. This involves discussions on short-term and long-term goals, market positioning, and competitive landscape analysis.

- **Strategic Context**

To ensure that the proposed solution aligns with the organization's strategic direction, it's essential to analyze how the project fits into the broader business context. This may involve conducting a SWOT analysis or PESTEL analysis to identify internal and external factors that could impact the project.

3.1.2. Identifying Functional and Non-Functional Requirements

In this section, we'll talk about two important types of requirements: functional and non-functional.

- **Functional Requirements**

Functional requirements outline the specific features and capabilities the solution must possess. These requirements are typically derived from discussions with end-users and stakeholders. They answer questions like "What should the system do?" and "How should it do it?"

- **Non-Functional Requirements**

Non-functional requirements encompass qualities the solution must possess, such as performance, security, usability, and scalability. It's vital to define metrics and benchmarks for each non-functional requirement to ensure they are measurable and achievable.

3.1.3. Strategic Stakeholder Identification and Engagement

Effective stakeholder engagement is crucial for project success. It starts with identifying stakeholders, establishing communication channels, and using various techniques to gather their requirements and insights.

- **Stakeholder Identification**

Identify all relevant stakeholders, including end-users, management, subject matter experts, and regulatory bodies. Develop a stakeholder matrix to categorize their interests, influence, and involvement in the project.

- **Communication Channels**

Establish clear and efficient communication channels with stakeholders. This may involve regular meetings, surveys, feedback mechanisms, or collaboration tools. Effective communication ensures that stakeholders are informed and engaged throughout the project lifecycle.

- **Requirements Elicitation**

Conduct interviews, workshops, surveys, or focus groups to elicit requirements and gather insights. Effective requirements elicitation techniques help in capturing both explicit and implicit stakeholder needs.

3.1.4. Evaluating Constraints and Assumptions

In the process, it's essential to evaluate constraints and assumptions. Constraints, like budget and time limitations, can significantly impact the project, while assumptions need to be validated to reduce potential risks. Let's explore how to effectively manage these critical aspects.

- **Constraint Analysis**

Identify and document constraints that might impact the project, such as budget limitations, time constraints, legal regulations, or technological limitations. Ensure that these constraints are understood and factored into the solution design.

- **Assumption Validation**

List and validate assumptions made during the requirement gathering phase. Assumptions should be tested for accuracy to minimize risks associated with erroneous assumptions.

3.2. Defining System Boundaries and Scope

3.2.1. Defining System Components

It involves identifying and defining major system parts based on functional requirements and simplifying complex components when necessary. Lets look into following two main aspects:

- **Component Identification**

Begin by identifying and defining the major components or modules that will constitute the system. These components should align with the functional requirements identified in the previous phase.

- **Functional Decomposition**

Decompose these components further into subcomponents or modules, as necessary. This process helps in breaking down complex systems into manageable and understandable parts.

3.2.2. Establishing Interfaces and Interaction Points

In this phase, we define component connections, specify data exchanges, and establish protocols for seamless communication. This phase has two key aspects,

- **Interface Definition**

Define the interfaces between system components or modules. This includes specifying the data, commands, or signals that are exchanged between components and how they interact.

- **Interaction Protocols**

Establish clear interaction protocols for the identified interfaces. This ensures that components can communicate seamlessly and that data flow is well-defined and reliable.

3.2.3. Identifying External Dependencies

In Identifying External Dependencies, we assess and manage external entities or systems, ensuring smooth integration and risk mitigation. Let dive into two key aspect of this phase,

- **Dependency Assessment**

Identify external entities or systems that the proposed system will interact with or depend upon. This may include external databases, third-party services, or legacy systems.

- **Dependency Management**

Develop strategies to manage and mitigate risks associated with external dependencies. This may involve contingency plans, data synchronization mechanisms, or service-level agreements (SLAs).

3.2.4. Clarifying System Responsibilities

This phase assigns roles and responsibilities to system components and establish error handling and exception management protocols. Now, let's explore the details of these responsibilities under Role Assignment and Error Handling.

- **Role Assignment**

Define the roles and responsibilities of each system component or module. Ensure that it's clear who is responsible for what within the system.

- **Error Handling and Exception Management**

Specify how the system should handle errors, exceptions, and unexpected behaviors. This includes defining error codes, error messages, and recovery procedures.

3.3. High-Level Architecture Design

3.3.1. Developing Conceptual Architecture

In High-Level Architecture Design, we create a Conceptual Architecture that outlines core principles and identifies key abstractions for the system.

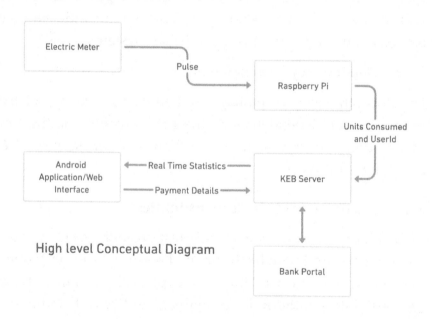

High level Conceptual Diagram

Let's now examine the Conceptual Framework and Key Abstractions in more detail.

- **Conceptual Framework**

Begin by creating a high-level conceptual framework for the system. This framework should capture the core concepts, principles, and goals that will guide the architecture design.

- **Key Abstractions**

Identify and define key abstractions or architectural concepts that will serve as building blocks for the system. These abstractions should align with the system's objectives and requirements.

3.3.2. Choosing Architectural Styles and Patterns

Choose styles and patterns based on project requirements and apply them to shape the system's design. Let's dive deeper into this process with a focus on Style Selection and Architectural Pattern Application.

- **Architectural Style Selection**

Evaluate various architectural styles (e.g., client-server, microservices, event-driven) and patterns (e.g., MVC, RESTful) to determine the most suitable ones for your project. Consider factors such as scalability, maintainability, and performance.

- **Architectural Pattern Application**

Apply selected architectural styles and patterns to shape the system's design. Define how these patterns will be implemented to address specific functional and non-functional requirements.

3.3.3. Defining Major Components and their Relationships

When defining major components and their relationships, we identify key system elements aligned with the chosen architecture and specify how they interact to achieve the system's goals. Next, let's examine Component Identification and Relationship Modeling in more detail.

- **Component Identification**

Identify the major components or modules that make up the system's architecture. These components should align with the conceptual framework and chosen architectural styles.

- **Relationship Modeling**

Define the relationships and interactions between these components. Determine how data, control, and communication flow between them to achieve the system's objectives.

3.3.4. Allocating Responsibilities to Components

In this section, we define each component's roles and functions and specify communication interfaces to enable seamless cooperation. Let's take a closer look at Responsibility Assignment and Interface Specification.

- **Responsibility Assignment**

Assign specific responsibilities and functions to each major component. Clearly define what each component is responsible for in terms of functionality and data processing.

- **Interface Specification**

Specify the interfaces between components, detailing the methods, parameters, and data formats used for communication. This ensures that components can work together seamlessly.

3.4. Creating Architecture Diagrams and System Flows

Architectural diagrams and data flow visualizations are essential tools for understanding, designing, and communicating the structure and behavior of complex systems. They provide a visual representation of how different components interact and how data flows through the system.

3.4.1. Flowcharts and Their Role in Visualization

Flowcharts are graphical representations of processes or workflows. They use various shapes to represent different types of **steps**, **decisions**, or **actions** within a process. **Arrows connect these shapes to indicate the flow or sequence of steps.** Flowcharts are widely used for business processes, software development, and system documentation. They play a crucial role in visualizing the flow of information or activities within a system, helping stakeholders understand complex processes.

Benefits of Flowchart:

- Simplifies complex system structures for easier understanding.

System Design Process

- Ensures a common and consistent method for expressing design concepts.

- Supports various diagram types for design, analysis, and documentation.

- Guides developers in translating design concepts into executable code.

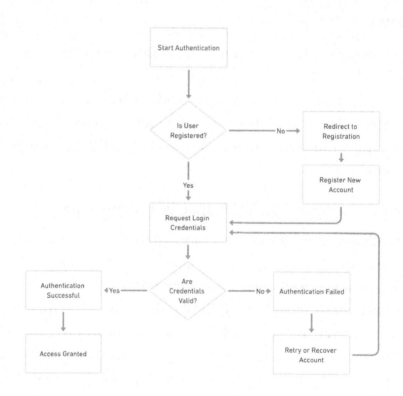

Flowchart

3.4.2. The C4 Model: Context, Containers, Components, Code

The C4 Model is a framework for visualizing the architecture of software systems. It is valuable for communicating the architecture of a system at different levels of abstraction.

It consists of four levels:

1. **Context Diagrams:** These provide a high-level view of the system, showing how it interacts with external entities or systems.

2. **Container Diagrams:** These focus on the containers (e.g., web servers, databases) that make up the system and how they interact.

3. **Component Diagrams:** These drill down further into individual components or services within containers, illustrating their interactions.

4. **Code Diagrams:** At the lowest level, these diagrams show the internal details of the components, such as classes, interfaces, and their relationships.

C4model itself explained those diagram in a great way, please check them out for more in detail view.
https://c4model.com/

3.4.3. Unified Modeling Language (UML) 2.5 Overview

Unified Modeling Language (UML) is a standardized modeling language used in software engineering. It provides a set of diagrams and notations to visually represent different aspects of a system. UML is widely used for designing and documenting software systems.

There are 14 types of UML diagrams falling into two main categories.

1. **Structural Diagrams**

2. **Behavioral Diagrams**

But we would discuss the most used diagrams

3.4.3.1. Structural Diagrams

1. **Class Diagram:** This diagram represents the static structure of a system, showing classes, their attributes, operations, and relationships. It is widely used in software design to illustrate data models and system architecture.

2. **Object Diagram:** It provides a snapshot of the system at a specific point in time, showing instances of classes and their relationships. This diagram is useful for visualizing and understanding system state and object interactions.

3. **Component Diagram:** This diagram depicts how components are wired together to form larger components or software systems. It focuses on the organization and wiring of the physical components in a system.

4. **Composite Structure Diagram:** It shows the internal structure of a class and the collaborations that this structure makes possible. This diagram is useful for understanding complex systems and software architecture.

5. **Deployment Diagram:** Models the physical deployment of artifacts on nodes, this diagram illustrates the hardware topology of a system, the distribution of software components, and their interactions.

6. **Package Diagram:** This diagram represents the organization of packages and their elements in a system. It is useful for managing dependencies and organizing elements in large systems or software.

7. **Profile Diagram:** It extends the UML by allowing the creation of custom stereotypes, tagged values, and constraints. This diagram is used to tailor UML models for specific domains or platforms.

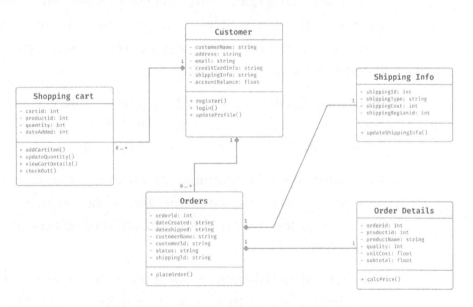

Class Diagram

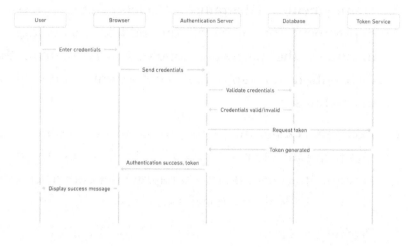

Sequence Diagram

3.4.3.2. Behavioral Diagrams

1. **Use Case Diagram:** This diagram represents the functionality of a system from an external point of view. It is useful for identifying and organizing system requirements.

2. **Sequence Diagram:** Shows how objects interact in a particular scenario of a use case. This diagram is useful for modeling the flow of messages in a system.

3. **Communication Diagram:** Illustrates the interactions between objects or parts in terms of sequenced messages. It focuses on the organization of objects and their links.

4. **State Machine Diagram:** Models the states of an object and the transitions that cause a change in state. This diagram is useful for modeling the behavior of an object throughout its lifecycle.

5. **Activity Diagram:** Represents the flow of control or data from activity to activity within a system. It is useful for modeling business processes and operational workflows.

6. **Interaction Overview Diagram:** Combines elements of activity and sequence diagrams to show a control flow with nodes that can contain interaction diagrams. This diagram is useful for providing an overview of complex control flows.

7. **Timing Diagram:** Focuses on the timing constraints and time ordering of messages and interactions. This diagram is useful for understanding and analyzing system behavior in terms of timing and durations.

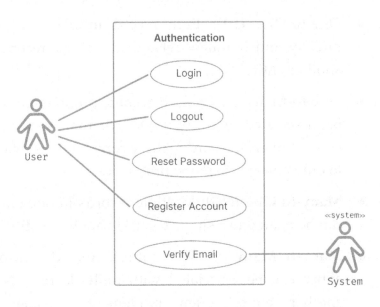

use case Diagram

3.4.4. Entity-Relationship Diagrams (ERD)

Entity-Relationship Diagrams (ERD) are a visual representation of the relationships among entities in a database. Entities are represented as rectangles, and relationships between them are depicted with lines. Key components include:

- **Entities:** Represent objects or concepts in the system.

- **Attributes:** Characteristics or properties of entities.

- **Relationships:** Connections between entities, indicating how they are related.

- ERDs are crucial for database design, helping to ensure that data is organized and relationships are well-defined. There are two types of relationships

  - **One-to-One (1:1):** Each record in one entity is directly and uniquely related to a single record in another entity.

  - **One-to-Many (1:N):** Each record in one entity can be associated with multiple records in another entity, but each record in the second entity is related to only one record in the first entity.

  - **Many-to-One (N:1):** Multiple records in one entity can be related to a single record in another entity.

  - **Many-to-Many (N:N):** Multiple records in one entity can be associated with multiple records in another entity, often implemented using an intermediate table.

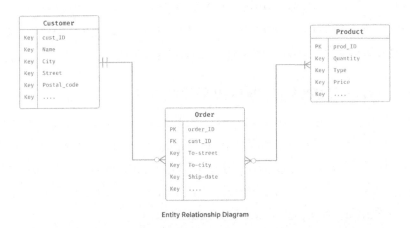

Entity Relationship Diagram

These visualization techniques and models are essential tools in software engineering and system design, providing a common language for communication among stakeholders.

3.5. Detailed Component Design and Specification

3.5.1. Refining Component Interfaces

When refining component interfaces, we provide detailed specifications for methods, parameters, and data structures while also implementing robust data validation and error-handling procedures at the interface level. Now, let's dive deeper into the specifics of Interface Refinement and Data Validation and Error Handling.

- **Interface Refinement**

In this stage, focus on refining and elaborating the interfaces between system components. Specify the methods, parameters, and data structures in greater detail.

- **Data Validation and Error Handling**

Define how input data is validated and how errors are handled at the interface level. Ensure robustness and resilience in handling unexpected scenarios.

3.5.2. Specifying Component Behaviors

In Specifying Component Behaviors, we detail each component's functions and operations, covering both functional and non-functional aspects. let's discuss the specifics of Functional Behavior Definition and Non-Functional Behavior Consideration.

- **Functional Behavior Definition**

Specify the detailed functional behavior of each component. Describe the algorithms, logic, and operations that each component performs to fulfill its responsibilities.

- **Non-Functional Behavior Consideration**

Address non-functional aspects of component behavior, including performance optimization, security measures, and compliance with quality attributes such as scalability and maintainability.

3.5.3. Designing Data Models and Schema

In the process of Designing Data Models and Schema, we develop comprehensive data structures and database schemas that correspond to these models. Let's deep dive into Data Model Creation and Schema Definition in more detail

- **Data Model Creation**

Develop detailed data models that define the structure and relationships of data entities within the system. Specify data attributes, constraints, and normalization techniques.

- **Schema Definition**

For database systems, create schema designs that reflect the data models. Specify tables, indexes, constraints, and data integrity rules.

3.5.4. Developing Algorithms and Procedures

In Developing Algorithms and Procedures, we design algorithms for data processing and outline step-by-step procedural flows for critical system processes. Now, let's look into Algorithm Design and Procedural Flow.

- **Algorithm Design**

Design algorithms and data processing procedures required for system functionality. Specify algorithmic approaches for data manipulation, calculations, and decision-making.

- **Procedural Flow**

Define the step-by-step procedural flow for critical processes within the system. Describe how data moves through the system and how actions are triggered.

3.6. Integration and Interface Design

3.6.1. Defining Integration Points and Protocols

In the phase of Defining Integration Points and Protocols, we identify where the system connects with external entities and define communication specifics, ensuring compatibility and, when applicable, adherence to industry standards. Now, let's look into the specifics of Integration Point Identification and Protocol Specification.

- **Integration Point Identification**

Identify the integration points where the proposed system interfaces with external entities, systems, or services. This includes both internal and external integration points.

- **Protocol Specification**

Specify the communication protocols, data formats, and message exchange patterns to be used for each integration point. Ensure compatibility and adherence to industry standards where applicable.

3.6.2. Designing API Contracts

In Designing API Contracts, we define API endpoints with clear details on methods and parameters. We also validate these contracts by documenting request-response formats, error codes, and authentication. Now, let's look into API Endpoint Definition and Contract Validation.

- **API Endpoint Definition**

Define the endpoints of any APIs (Application Programming Interfaces) that are part of the system. Clearly outline the methods, endpoints, and parameters.

- **Contract Validation**

Ensure that API contracts are well-documented and validated. This involves specifying request and response formats, error codes, and authentication mechanisms.

3.6.3. Specifying Communication Methods

In this phase, we select appropriate technologies for integration points and decide on synchronous or asynchronous communication based on data exchange and performance requirements. Now, let's discuss Communication Channel Selection and Synchronous vs. Asynchronous decisions.

- **Communication Channel Selection**

Select the appropriate communication methods for different integration points. This may include RESTful APIs, message queues, WebSocket, or other suitable technologies.

- **Asynchronous vs. Synchronous**

Determine whether communication should be synchronous or asynchronous, depending on the nature of the data exchange and the system's performance requirements.

3.6.4. Ensuring Data Consistency across Interfaces

In Ensuring Data Consistency across Interfaces, we establish strategies for data integrity and synchronization, handling conflicts, and managing errors effectively. let's explore Data Synchronization and Error Handling and Recovery in more detail.

- **Data Synchronization:**

Define strategies for data consistency and synchronization across interfaces. This includes handling data conflicts, ensuring data integrity, and maintaining referential integrity.

- **Error Handling and Recovery**

Specify how errors and exceptions will be managed across interfaces. Define error codes, retry mechanisms, and fault tolerance strategies.

3.7. Security and Compliance Considerations

3.7.1. Identifying Security Requirements

In Identifying Security Requirements, we analyze project-specific security needs, assess threats and risks, and define clear security goals, including confidentiality, integrity, and availability. let's discuss Requirement Analysis and Security Goal Definition.

- **Requirement Analysis**

Conduct a comprehensive analysis to identify security requirements specific to the project. This involves assessing potential threats, vulnerabilities, and risks.

- **Security Goals**

Define clear security goals, such as confidentiality, integrity, and availability, based on the organization's needs and industry standards.

3.7.2. Defining Authentication and Authorization

In defining Authentication and Authorization, we specify user authentication methods and create an access control framework, defining roles and permissions. Let's now explore Authentication Mechanisms and Authorization Framework in more depth.

- **Authentication Mechanisms**

Specify the methods and mechanisms for user authentication. This may include single sign-on (SSO), multi-factor authentication (MFA), or biometric authentication.

- **Authorization Framework**

Design an authorization framework that governs access to system resources. Define roles, permissions, and access control lists (ACLs) to ensure proper authorization.

3.7.3. Ensuring Data Privacy and Integrity

In Ensuring Data Privacy and Integrity, we safeguard data through encryption (e.g., TLS/SSL) for transit and storage, and we also protect sensitive information using data masking, redaction, or anonymization strategies.

- **Data Encryption**

Implement data encryption techniques (e.g., TLS/SSL) to protect data in transit and at rest. Define encryption algorithms and key management practices.

- **Data Masking and Redaction**

Determine how sensitive data is handled and protected within the system. Specify data masking, redaction, or anonymization strategies to safeguard privacy.

3.7.4. Addressing Regulatory and Compliance Needs

In Addressing Regulatory and Compliance Needs, we assess alignment with regulations like GDPR or HIPAA and define Compliance Controls, including audit trails and reporting.

Let's explore Compliance Assessment and Compliance Controls further.

- **Compliance Assessment**

Identify relevant regulatory requirements and compliance standards (e.g., GDPR, HIPAA, PCI DSS). Assess how the system design aligns with these standards.

- **Compliance Controls**

Specify compliance controls and measures to ensure adherence to regulations. Develop audit trails, logging mechanisms, and reporting capabilities as needed.

3.8. Scalability, Performance, and Reliability Design

3.8.1. Planning for Scalability and Load Balancing

In Planning for Scalability and Load Balancing, we assess expected growth, identify bottlenecks, and plan for scaling, while also defining load balancing strategies to distribute traffic across servers. Now, let's dive into Scalability Assessment and Load Balancing Strategy.

- **Scalability Assessment**

Evaluate the expected growth and usage patterns of the system. Identify scalability bottlenecks and plan for horizontal or vertical scaling as needed.

- **Load Balancing Strategy**

Define load balancing strategies to evenly distribute incoming traffic across multiple servers or instances. Specify algorithms (e.g., round-robin, least connections) and load balancing mechanisms.

3.8.2. Optimizing Performance and Resource Utilization

In the context of Performance and Resource Optimization, we begin with Performance Profiling to identify critical components and areas needing improvement. We then move on to Performance Optimization, where we apply techniques like caching, indexing, and query optimization to enhance system responsiveness. Let's look into Performance Profiling and Performance Optimization.

- **Performance Profiling**

Conduct performance profiling and analysis to identify performance-critical components and areas of improvement.

- **Performance Optimization**

Implement performance optimization techniques, such as caching, indexing, compression, and query optimization, to enhance system responsiveness.

3.8.3. Designing for Fault Tolerance and Recovery

In Designing for Fault Tolerance and Recovery, we identify failure points and establish fault tolerance measures like redundancy and failover. We also create disaster recovery plans for data and service continuity during major failures. Explore the Fault Tolerance Measures and Disaster Recovery Planning further.

- **Fault Tolerance Measures**

Identify potential failure points in the system and design fault tolerance mechanisms. This may include redundancy, failover, and graceful degradation strategies.

- **Disaster Recovery Planning**

Develop disaster recovery plans and procedures to ensure data and service continuity in the event of major failures or disasters.

3.8.4. Ensuring System Reliability and Availability

- **Reliability Modeling**

Model system reliability by calculating Mean Time Between Failures (MTBF) and Mean Time To Recovery (MTTR). Define reliability targets based on business needs.

- **High Availability Architecture**

Design a high availability architecture with redundancy and failover mechanisms to minimize downtime and ensure continuous availability.

3.9. Validation, Verification, and Testing

3.9.1. Reviewing Architectural Decisions

In this process, we calculate system reliability metrics and set targets based on business needs. We also design a High Availability Architecture with redundancy and failover to minimize downtime. Next, let's look into Reliability Modeling and High Availability Architecture.

- **Architecture Review**: Conduct a comprehensive review of architectural decisions made throughout the design process. Ensure alignment with requirements, best practices, and design principles.

- **Stakeholder Feedback:** Collect feedback from stakeholders, including technical experts and business representatives. Address any concerns, risks, or recommendations related to the architecture.

- **Architecture Decision Records (ADR):** Document key architectural decisions made during the project. This includes the context, decision, and rationale. Ensure that ADRs are accessible and maintained for future reference and accountability. Regularly review and update ADRs to reflect evolving project needs and lessons learned.

3.9.2. Conducting Design Verifications

In Conducting Design Verifications, we verify the detailed design's alignment with high-level architecture and specifications, ensuring consistency with the original goals. We also assess potential design risks and develop mitigation plans. Next, let's look into Design Compliance and Risk Assessment.

- **Design Compliance**

Verify that the detailed design adheres to the high-level architecture and design specifications. Check for consistency and alignment with the original design goals.

- **Risk Assessment**

Assess potential design risks and their impact on the project. Develop mitigation plans for identified risks.

3.9.3. Performing Component and Integration Testing

In Performing Component and Integration Testing, we start with Component Testing to check individual components' functionality. Then, we conduct Integration Testing to validate interactions and data flow between components.

- **Component Testing**

Execute unit and component tests to verify the functionality and behavior of individual components. Ensure that each component operates correctly in isolation.

- **Integration Testing**

Conduct integration testing to validate the interaction and compatibility of integrated components. Verify that data flows smoothly between components and that interfaces work as expected.

3.9.4. Collecting Feedback and Refining the Architecture

In this process, we gather testing feedback, document issues, and use this feedback iteratively to enhance the architecture and improve system quality. Now, let's discuss Test Feedback and Iterative Refinement.

- **Test Feedback**

Collect feedback and results from testing efforts. Identify and document defects, performance issues, or unexpected behaviors.

- **Iterative Refinement**

Use the feedback obtained to refine the architecture as needed. Make necessary adjustments to address identified issues and enhance overall system quality.

3.10. Documentation and Knowledge Transfer

3.10.1. Creating Comprehensive Architectural Documentation

In this phase, we establish standards and templates for consistency. We then provide thorough documentation, covering architectural decisions, components, interfaces, data models, and non-functional requirements.

- **Documentation Standards**

Establish clear documentation standards and templates to ensure consistency and completeness in documenting the architecture.

- **Documenting Design**

Document the architecture comprehensively, including high-level and detailed design documents, diagrams, and models. This should cover architectural decisions, components, interfaces, data models, and non-functional requirements.

3.10.2. Communicating Design Decisions to Stakeholders

In Communicating Design Decisions to Stakeholders, we engage stakeholders through meetings and provide insights into design rationale. We address concerns and align the design with business objectives. Now, let's explore this phase in more detail, covering Stakeholder Engagement and Addressing Concerns.

- **Stakeholder Engagement**

Engage with stakeholders to communicate design decisions effectively. Hold meetings, presentations, or workshops to ensure that stakeholders understand the rationale behind the architecture.

- **Addressing Concerns**

Be prepared to address questions, concerns, and feedback from stakeholders. Provide clarification and insights into how the design aligns with business objectives.

3.10.3. Providing Guidance for Implementation and Maintenance

In Guiding Implementation and Maintenance, we offer implementation guidelines and outline maintenance strategies, ensuring architecture supports ease of maintenance and scalability. Let's discuss Implementation Guidelines and Maintenance Strategies in more detail.

- **Implementation Guidelines**

Create guidelines and best practices documentation to assist development teams in implementing the design. Provide coding standards, patterns, and frameworks as applicable.

- **Maintenance Strategies**

Outline strategies for system maintenance, including updates, patches, and bug fixes. Document how the architecture supports easy maintenance and scalability.

3.10.4. Ensuring Future Adaptability and Extendibility

In Ensuring Future Adaptability and Extendibility, we plan for design evolution to meet evolving needs and create an extensibility framework for future enhancements and technology integration. Now, let's look into Design Evolution and the Extensibility Framework.

- **Design Evolution**

Describe strategies for evolving the architecture over time to meet changing business requirements and technological advancements.

- **Extensibility Framework**

Define an extensibility framework that allows for future feature enhancements and integration of new technologies without major architectural overhauls.

CHAPTER 4

DATABASES AND DATA MANAGEMENT

CHAPTER 4:

DATABASES AND DATA MANAGEMENT

In the dynamic world of technology, databases stand as the backbone of information storage and retrieval. However, a common pitfall in many projects is the selection of a database system without a thorough understanding of its alignment with business needs. This chapter, "Databases and Data Management," is crafted to address this critical aspect of system design and to guide you in making informed decisions about database selection and data management strategies.

The choice of a database can significantly impact the performance, scalability, and efficiency of a system. For instance, using a SQL database for IoT device data might seem adequate initially, but as the volume and velocity of data increase, a time-series database becomes a more suitable choice. Similarly, opting for a NoSQL database in scenarios that require high relational data handling can lead to complications, where a graph or SQL database would be the optimal solution. These examples underscore the importance of selecting the right database based on specific use cases and data characteristics.

As systems evolve and data grows exponentially, the initial choice of a database may no longer suffice. A common scenario is the use of a SQL database for all data storage and retrieval tasks, which can lead to performance bottlenecks, such as slow response times or timeouts during searches. In such cases, integrating a specialized database like Elasticsearch for search operations can dramatically improve performance. This chapter will explore various database types, including relational, NoSQL, time-series, graph, and distributed databases, and specialized types, each suited for different scenarios.

Furthermore, we explore strategies for optimizing data retrieval. Caching stands out as a crucial technique to reduce database load and enhance retrieval speed. Knowing when and how to implement caching can greatly improve system performance and user experience.

Another crucial concept covered in this chapter is the CAP theorem, which provides a framework for understanding the trade-offs between consistency, availability, and partition tolerance in distributed systems. This theorem is instrumental in guiding the choice of database type, especially in complex, distributed environments.

The chapter is structured to provide a comprehensive understanding of databases and data management:

- **Introduction to Databases:** Understanding the characteristics and purposes of databases.

- **Types of Databases:** Exploring various database types and their specific use cases.

- **Choosing the Right Database for Your System:** Applying the CAP theorem and understanding trade-offs.

- **Designing Robust Databases:** Steps to create a well-structured and efficient database.

- **Optimizing Data Retrieval:** Techniques like searching, indexing, and caching.

- **Challenges and Future Trends:** Addressing current challenges and anticipating future developments in database technology.

By the end of this chapter, you will have a clear understanding of how to select the appropriate database for your system's needs, design robust database structures, and implement effective data retrieval and management strategies. This knowledge is crucial in ensuring that your system remains scalable, efficient, and aligned with evolving business requirements.

4.1. Introduction to Databases

A database is an organized collection of data that is stored electronically. It is designed to allow users to easily access, manipulate, and update the data. It serves as a central repository for storing, managing, and retrieving data for various applications and purposes. Databases are a fundamental component of modern information systems and play a crucial role in data management.

4.1.1. Database Characteristics

- **Data Structure**

Databases organize data in a structured format. The structure is typically defined using a data model, which specifies how data elements are related to each other. Common data models include relational, hierarchical, network, and document-oriented.

- **Data Integrity**

Databases enforce data integrity constraints to maintain the accuracy and consistency of data. This includes ensuring that data meets specified validation rules and constraints, such as unique keys and foreign key relationships.

- **Enhanced Data Accessibility with DBMS Queries**

Before the introduction of Database Management Systems (DBMS), complex and extensive data were typically stored in conventional file systems, consisting of files and folders. Locating a specific piece of information, such as a student's name among thousands of records, proved to be a challenging task in this manual system. This difficulty arose from the need to manually search through files to locate the desired data.

In contrast, DBMS offers a significant improvement in terms of data accessibility. It allows users to effortlessly access data within the database by executing search queries. This querying process is not only substantially faster than manual searching but also more dependable and efficient.

- **Support for multiple views of data**

A database supports multiple views of data. A view is a subset of the database, which is defined and dedicated for particular users of the system. Multiple users in the system might have different views of the system. Each view might contain only the data of interest to a user or group of users.

- **Security**

Databases can be configured to protect data from unauthorized access and modification. This is important for sensitive data, such as financial data or medical records.

- **ACID Properties**

Databases typically adhere to the ACID (Atomicity, Consistency, Isolation, Durability) properties to ensure reliable and predictable data transactions.

- **Scalability**

Databases can be designed to scale horizontally (adding more servers or nodes) or vertically (upgrading hardware resources) to handle increased data volumes and user loads.

4.2. Types of Databases

4.2.1. Relational Databases

Relational databases are structured databases that store data in tables with predefined schemas. Each row in a table represents a record, and each column represents an attribute.

Characteristics

- **Structured Data:** Data in relational databases is structured, meaning it follows a fixed schema, and all data must fit this schema.

- **SQL:** They use SQL (Structured Query Language) for querying and manipulation.

- **ACID Properties:** Relational databases adhere to ACID properties, ensuring data consistency and integrity even in the face of system failures.

- **Joins:** They support complex queries involving JOIN operations to combine data from multiple tables.

- **Normalization:** Relational databases encourage data normalization to minimize redundancy and maintain data integrity.

Use Cases

- **Complex Queries:** Suitable for applications requiring complex queries, reporting, and data analysis, such as banking systems.

- **Data Integrity:** Ideal for scenarios where data integrity and consistency are paramount, like healthcare records.

Pros

- **Data Integrity:** ACID transactions guarantee data consistency.

- **Structured Data:** Ideal for structured data with well-defined relationships.

- **Mature Technology:** Widely adopted and mature technology with extensive tooling and support.

Cons

- **Scalability:** Scaling relational databases can be challenging for high-traffic applications.

- **Schema Changes:** Adapting to schema changes can be cumbersome.

4.2.2. NoSQL Databases

NoSQL (Not Only SQL) databases are designed for handling various types of unstructured or semi-structured data, offering greater flexibility and scalability.

Characteristics:

- **Flexible Schema:** NoSQL databases allow dynamic changes to data structures, making them suitable for rapidly evolving data.

- **High Scalability:** They excel at horizontal scalability, allowing them to handle large amounts of data and high traffic.

- **Variety of Models:** NoSQL databases support different data models, including document, key-value, column-family, and graph.

Use Cases:

- **Rapid Development:** Ideal for startups and projects where rapid development and flexibility are priorities.

- **Big Data:** Suited for applications dealing with big data, like social media platforms or streaming services.

Comparison with Relational Databases

- **Schema Flexibility:** NoSQL databases are more adaptable to changing data structures.

- **Scalability:** NoSQL databases are often more scalable horizontally, making them suitable for web-scale applications.

4.2.3. Time Series Databases

Time series databases are optimized for storing and querying time-stamped data points, such as sensor readings, stock prices, or IoT telemetry.

Characteristics:

- **Time-Ordered Data:** They organize data based on timestamps, enabling efficient retrieval of historical data.

- **Aggregation:** Support for aggregating and summarizing time series data for analytics.

- **Data Compression:** Time series databases often employ data compression techniques to save storage space.

Use Cases:

- **IoT Data:** Ideal for storing and analyzing data from sensors, devices, and IoT applications.

- **Monitoring Systems:** Used in monitoring and alerting systems for real-time analytics.

4.2.4. Graph Databases

Graph databases store data as nodes (entities) and edges (relationships), making them highly efficient for querying and traversing complex, interconnected data.

Characteristics

- **Graph Structure:** Data is modeled as a graph, enabling efficient representation of relationships.

- **Query Language:** They often come with specialized query languages (e.g., Cypher for Neo4j) for graph traversal.

- **Complex Queries:** Ideal for complex queries involving pathfinding, recommendation engines, or social network analysis.

Use Cases:

- **Social Networks:** Graph databases are used to model and query social connections.

- **Recommendation Engines:** Ideal for building recommendation systems based on user interactions and preferences.

4.2.5. Distributed Databases

Distributed databases span multiple servers or locations, providing high availability and fault tolerance by distributing data across nodes.

Characteristics

- **Data Replication:** Data is often replicated across multiple nodes for redundancy.

- **Fault Tolerance:** Distributed databases can withstand node failures without data loss.

- **Scalability:** They allow horizontal scalability to handle growing workloads.

Use Cases:

- **Global Services:** Suitable for services that need to be available worldwide, such as e-commerce websites.

- **High Availability:** Used in systems where downtime is unacceptable, like financial institutions.

4.2.6. Specialized Database Types

These databases store data as objects, mirroring object-oriented programming concepts. They are used in applications where complex data models need to be represented, such as computer-aided design (CAD) systems.

- **Document Stores:** Document databases, like MongoDB, store data in flexible, JSON-like documents. They are well-suited for semi-structured data and content management systems.

- **Key-Value Stores:** Key-value stores, such as Redis, store data as simple key-value pairs, making them extremely fast and efficient for caching and real-time data needs.

4.3. Choosing Right Database for your System

Choosing the right database for a specific application involves considering various factors, including the application's requirements, scalability needs, and the desired trade-offs between consistency, availability, and partition tolerance. The CAP theorem can be a useful guide in making informed decisions about the database architecture.

4.3.1. CAP Theorem

The CAP theorem, proposed by computer scientist Eric Brewer, helps guide decisions about the design and implementation of distributed databases. It states that in a distributed system, you can achieve at most two out of the three desirable properties: Consistency, Availability, and Partition Tolerance.

Let's break down each component:

- **Consistency (C):** This implies that all nodes in a distributed system see the same data at the same time. In other words, when a write is completed, all subsequent reads will return the most recent write. Achieving strong consistency may involve waiting for acknowledgments from multiple nodes, which can impact system performance.

- **Availability (A):** This means that every request to the system gets a response, without guarantee that it contains the most recent version of the information. High availability is crucial for systems that require continuous operation, even in the face of failures.

- **Partition Tolerance (P):** This refers to the system's ability to continue functioning even if communication between nodes is lost or delayed. In a distributed system, partitions (communication failures) are inevitable, so it's essential to be able to tolerate them.

In essence, the CAP theorem asserts that in the event of a network partition, you must choose between maintaining consistency or availability.

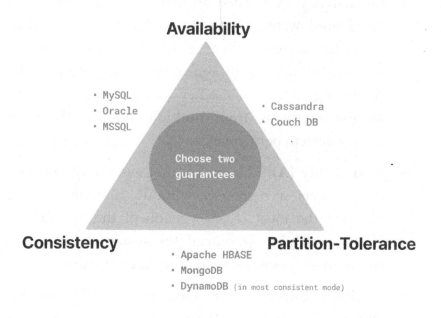

Availability

• MySQL
• Oracle
• MSSQL

• Cassandra
• Couch DB

Choose two
guarantees

Consistency   **Partition-Tolerance**

• Apache HBASE
• MongoDB
• DynamoDB (in most consistent mode)

CAP Theorem

4.3.1.1. Trade-offs:

- **CA (Consistency and Availability, no Partition Tolerance):** In a non-partitioned system, you can achieve both consistency and availability. However, in the presence of network partitions, the system must sacrifice either consistency or availability.

- **CP (Consistency and Partition Tolerance, no Availability):** In this case, the system chooses consistency over availability in the face of a partition. This means that the system may become temporarily unavailable during a partition.

- **AP (Availability and Partition Tolerance, no Consistency):** This scenario sacrifices consistency in favor of availability and partition tolerance. The system continues to function even if the nodes are not in sync.

When selecting a database, consider your application's requirements and the trade-offs you are willing to make. Some databases are designed with a focus on consistency (e.g., traditional relational databases), while others prioritize availability and partition tolerance (e.g., NoSQL databases like Cassandra or Couchbase). Understanding the CAP theorem can help you make informed decisions based on your specific use case and requirements.

4.4. Designing Robust Databases

Database design is the foundational process of creating a structured and efficient system for storing and managing data. In the digital age, data is at the heart of almost every aspect of business and technology. Whether it's customer information, financial records, product catalogs, or more, a well-designed database is the cornerstone of effective data management. A thoughtfully crafted database ensures that data is not only organized logically but is also easily accessible, secure, and capable of adapting to evolving needs. Database design encompasses a series of critical steps and principles that aim to optimize data integrity, performance, and flexibility. In this discussion, we will explore the key components and best practices involved in creating a robust and purpose-driven database, setting the stage for efficient data management and informed decision-making.

4.4.1. Determining the Purpose of Your Database

- Start by defining the purpose and objectives of your database. Consider why you need the database and what you aim to achieve with it. For example, if you're designing a customer relationship management (CRM) database, your goal might be to track customer interactions and improve customer service.

- Understand the specific requirements and the scope of data you'll be dealing with. This could include data about customers, products, sales, or any other relevant information.

- Clearly defining the purpose of the database helps in setting the right direction for the design process and ensures that you capture all the essential data.

4.4.2. Finding and Organizing the Required Information

- Once you know the purpose, identify the data elements or attributes that need to be stored in your database. For a CRM database, this could include customer names, contact information, purchase history, and support ticket records.

- Organize these data elements into logical groups or categories. Grouping related data together simplifies the database structure and makes it easier to manage. For instance, you might create tables for customers, products, and orders.

- Determine how these data elements relate to one another. For the CRM database, you'll establish connections between customer records and their related orders and support tickets, forming a web of relationships.

4.4.3. Dividing the Information into Tables:

- With data elements identified and organized, create separate tables for each logical group or entity. Each table should have a clear and distinct purpose.

- For a CRM database, you might have separate tables for customers, products, orders, and support tickets. These tables will hold data specific to their respective entities.

- Dividing data into tables not only organizes the information but also ensures that you don't repeat the same data in multiple places (redundancy).

4.4.4. Turning Information Items into Columns:

- Define the specific attributes or columns within each table. These columns should represent the properties or characteristics of the entity.

- In the "Customers" table, you might have columns like customer ID, name, email, phone number, and address. In the "Products" table, columns may include product ID, name, description, price, etc.

- Carefully choose and name columns to accurately capture the essential information while avoiding unnecessary or redundant data.

4.4.5. Specifying Primary Keys:

- A primary key uniquely identifies each record in a table. It ensures data integrity and enables efficient data retrieval.

- In the "Customers" table, you might designate the customer ID as the primary key. This means that no two customers can have the same customer ID.

- Primary keys play a critical role in maintaining the uniqueness and consistency of data within a table.

4.4.6. Creating the Table Relationships:

- Establish relationships between tables to define how data in one table is connected to data in another.

- For instance, the "Customers" table can be linked to the "Orders" table through the customer's unique identifier. This relationship allows you to associate each order with a specific customer.

- Relationships are vital for complex data retrieval and maintaining data consistency across the database.

4.4.7. Refining the Design:

- After the initial design, gather feedback from users and stakeholders. Conduct thorough testing to identify any issues or areas for improvement.

- Adjust the design as necessary based on feedback and testing results. This refinement phase ensures that the database design aligns with the practical needs of the organization.

- It's an iterative process that may involve revisiting previous steps to optimize the design further.

4.4.8. Applying the Normalization Rules:

- Normalization is the process of organizing data in a way that reduces redundancy and enhances data integrity.

- Follow normalization rules like First Normal Form (1NF), Second Normal Form (2NF), and Third Normal Form (3NF) to structure the data efficiently.

- For example, in 1NF, ensure that each column holds atomic (indivisible) values, and in 2NF, eliminate partial dependencies within tables. This helps prevent data anomalies and supports efficient data management.

4.5. Optimizing Data Retrieval

Optimizing data retrieval is crucial for efficient and responsive applications. This involves strategies for searching, indexing, and choosing appropriate data stores.

4.5.1. Searching and Indexing

1. Indexing Strategies and Full-Text Search Techniques

Indexing is the process of creating data structures to speed up data retrieval.

Common indexing techniques include:

- **B-Tree indexes:** Ideal for range queries on data with a natural order.

- **Hash indexes:** Efficient for exact match lookups.

- **Bitmap indexes:** Useful for low-cardinality data like gender or status flags.

- Full-text search techniques involve text-based search within documents or unstructured data.

- **Inverted index:** A data structure to speed up text-based search.

- **Tokenization:** Breaking text into tokens for efficient searching.

- **Stemming and lemmatization:** Reducing words to their root form to enhance search accuracy.

2. Optimizing Search: Best Practices

Some of the best practices to optimize searches are,

- **Query optimization:** Techniques to enhance the efficiency of search queries.

- **Query rewriting:** Transforming complex queries into simpler, equivalent forms.

- **Query caching:** Storing frequently used query results for rapid retrieval.

- **Relevance ranking:** Assigning scores to search results based on their relevance.

- **Faceted search:** Providing filters for users to narrow down search results.

- **Monitoring and profiling:** Tracking query performance and identifying bottlenecks for optimization.

3. Data Stores for Searching

Selecting the appropriate data store is a crucial aspect of optimizing data retrieval, especially when it comes to searching. Different data stores have varying strengths and weaknesses, and the choice often depends on the specific requirements of the application. Here are some popular data stores used for searching:

Elasticsearch: is a specialized search engine that excels at full-text search and real-time analytics. It is built on top of Apache Lucene and is highly scalable. Elasticsearch supports complex queries, filtering, and relevance ranking, making it an excellent choice for applications with heavy search requirements.

OpenSearch: OpenSearch is a distributed search and analytics engine that forked from Elasticsearch. It is fully open source and aims to maintain transparency and community-driven development. OpenSearch continues to provide powerful search capabilities similar to Elasticsearch.

Apache Solr: Similar to Elasticsearch, Apache Solr is an open-source search platform built on Apache Lucene. It provides features like faceted search, distributed search, and indexing. Solr is known for its robustness in handling large volumes of textual data.

MeiliSearch: It is a fast, open-source search engine designed for developers. It is known for its simplicity, ease of use, and real-time search capabilities. MeiliSearch is particularly suitable for small to medium-sized projects and offers features like typo-tolerance, filtering, and faceted search.

4.6. Challenges and Future Trends

4.6.1. Overview of Current Challenges:

Scalability: As the volume of data continues to grow exponentially, the scalability of databases becomes a significant challenge. Traditional relational databases may struggle to handle the sheer size and complexity of modern datasets. Scalable solutions, including distributed databases and cloud-based services, are increasingly vital.

Data Security and Privacy: With the rise of cyber threats and stringent data protection regulations, ensuring the security and privacy of sensitive information is a critical challenge. Data breaches can lead to severe consequences, including financial losses and damage to an organization's reputation.

Complexity of Querying and Analysis: As datasets become more extensive and more complex, the ability to query and analyze data efficiently becomes challenging. Users demand faster query response times and more sophisticated analytics. This requires advanced indexing, optimization techniques, and the use of specialized databases tailored for analytics.

Data Governance and Compliance: Compliance with regulations such as GDPR, HIPAA, and others requires robust data governance practices. Ensuring that data is used ethically, is accurate, and meets regulatory requirements is an ongoing challenge for organizations.

4.6.2. Future of Databases and Data Management:

Distributed Ledger Technology (DLT) and Blockchain: The adoption of blockchain and distributed ledger technology is expected to increase for ensuring transparent and tamper-resistant data management. Blockchain provides a decentralized and secure way of recording and verifying transactions, making it suitable for applications like supply chain management and financial transactions.

Quantum Databases: The advent of quantum computing poses both challenges and opportunities for databases. Quantum databases are being explored to leverage the unique capabilities of quantum computers for solving complex problems, including optimization and cryptography.

Edge Computing and Edge Databases: With the proliferation of IoT devices and the need for low-latency processing, edge computing is gaining prominence. Edge databases are designed to operate closer to the data source, reducing latency and improving efficiency. This trend is particularly crucial for applications requiring real-time insights.

AI and Machine Learning Integration: The integration of artificial intelligence (AI) and machine learning (ML) into databases is expected to enhance automation, predictive analytics, and data processing capabilities. Intelligent databases can optimize performance, automate routine tasks, and provide insights based on patterns and trends within the data.

CHAPTER 5

CLOUD SOLUTIONS AND INFRASTRUCTURE

CHAPTER 5:

CLOUD SOLUTIONS AND

INFRASTRUCTURE

In the modern era of technology, where scalability and flexibility are paramount, Cloud Solutions and Infrastructure have emerged as key enablers in the design of scalable systems. This chapter aims to provide a comprehensive overview of how cloud technologies and infrastructure play a pivotal role in building systems that are not only efficient and robust but also capable of adapting to changing demands and scaling requirements.

The adoption of cloud solutions is a strategic decision for any organization aiming to build scalable systems. Cloud platforms offer unparalleled flexibility, allowing systems to scale resources up or down based on real-time demands. This elasticity is crucial for handling varying workloads, ensuring that systems remain both responsive and cost-effective.

We begin by exploring the modern cloud landscape, which is broadly categorized into Infrastructure as a Service (IaaS), Platform as a Service (PaaS), and Software as a Service (SaaS). Each model offers different levels of control, management, and scalability, catering to diverse business needs.

- **IaaS** provides fundamental computing resources over the internet, offering flexibility and scalability in managing hardware resources.

- **PaaS** offers a platform allowing customers to develop, run, and manage applications without the complexity of building and maintaining the infrastructure.

- **SaaS** delivers software applications over the internet, eliminating the need for installations and maintenance, thus offering scalability and ease of use.

The chapter also highlights the significance of Linux and Bash in the realm of open-source solutions, which form the backbone of many cloud infrastructures. Their versatility and robustness make them ideal for scalable system environments.

Next, we explore containerization and orchestration, focusing on Docker and Kubernetes. Containerization with Docker encapsulates applications in containers, ensuring consistency across multiple development and release cycles. Kubernetes, an orchestration tool, manages these containers, automating deployment, scaling, and operations of application containers across clusters of hosts.

We then examine resource provisioning tools like CloudFormation and Terraform, which automate the setup of cloud infrastructure, thereby reducing manual errors and increasing efficiency. The chapter discusses their use cases, key concepts, and how to choose between them.

Automation and resource management are critical in scalable systems, and Ansible plays a significant role in this area. We explore how Ansible can automate cloud and infrastructure services, enhancing the system's scalability and reliability.

Finally, the chapter discusses the role of managed services in scalable systems. Managed services offload specific IT operations to a service provider, allowing businesses to focus on their core functions while ensuring their IT infrastructure scales and evolves as needed.

5.1. Modern Cloud Landscape: IaaS, PaaS, and SaaS

The modern cloud computing landscape is characterized by three fundamental service models: **Infrastructure as a Service (IaaS)**, **Platform as a Service (PaaS)**, and **Software as a Service (SaaS)**. Each of these models provides distinct benefits and addresses specific aspects of an organization's IT infrastructure needs.

5.1.1. Infrastructure as a Service (IaaS):

It delivers fundamental computing resources over the internet, providing virtualized computing infrastructure. It includes services like virtual machines, storage, and networking.

Key Features:

- **Scalability:** Users can scale resources up or down based on demand without the need for physical hardware changes.

- **Flexibility:** Users have control over the operating system, applications, and runtime, allowing for a high degree of customization.

- **Pay-as-You-Go Model:** Users pay for the resources they consume on a usage basis, which can be cost-effective for variable workloads.

Use Cases:

- Development and Testing Environments

- Hosting Websites and Applications

- Disaster Recovery

Examples of IaaS Providers:

- Amazon Web Services (AWS) EC2

- Microsoft Azure Virtual Machines

- Google Cloud Compute Engine

5.1.2. Platform as a Service (PaaS):

It provides a higher-level platform that abstracts away the underlying infrastructure, offering a ready-to-use development and deployment environment.

Key Features:

- Simplified Development: Developers can focus on coding and application logic without managing the underlying infrastructure.

- Automatic Scaling: PaaS platforms often offer automatic scaling based on demand, ensuring optimal performance.

- Built-in Services: PaaS platforms typically include built-in services such as databases, messaging, and application hosting.

Use Cases:

- Application Development and Deployment

- Web Application Hosting

- Mobile App Development

Examples of PaaS Providers:

- Heroku

- Google App Engine

- Microsoft Azure App Service

5.1.3. Software as a Service (SaaS):

It delivers fully functional software applications over the internet, eliminating the need for users to install, maintain, and manage the software locally.

Key Features:

- Accessibility: Users can access the software through a web browser, often from any device with internet connectivity.

- Automatic Updates: SaaS providers handle maintenance, updates, and patches, ensuring users always have access to the latest features and security improvements.

- Subscription Model: Users typically pay a subscription fee, and the software is hosted centrally.

Use Cases:

- Email and Collaboration Tools

- Customer Relationship Management (CRM)

- Enterprise Resource Planning (ERP)

Examples of SaaS Providers:

- Salesforce

- Microsoft 365 (formerly Office 365)

- Dropbox

Integration Across Service Models:

- **Hybrid Cloud:** Organizations often adopt a hybrid cloud approach, combining on-premises infrastructure with public and private cloud services. This allows for flexibility and the ability to address specific business requirements.

- **Multi-Cloud:** Some organizations choose to use multiple cloud providers for different services, applications, or geographic regions to avoid vendor lock-in and enhance resilience.

5.2. Linux and Bash

Linux: It is a powerful and open-source operating system kernel that serves as the foundation for a variety of operating systems. It's part of the Unix-like family of operating systems and is widely used for servers, embedded systems, and as an alternative to proprietary operating systems.

Key Characteristics:

- **Open Source:** Linux's source code is freely available, allowing users to view, modify, and distribute their versions. This open nature encourages collaboration and innovation.

- **Multiuser and Multitasking:** Linux supports multiple users simultaneously, each running multiple processes. This capability makes it suitable for both personal and enterprise use.

- **Stability and Reliability:** Linux is known for its stability and reliability. Systems running Linux often have long uptimes without the need for frequent reboots.

- **Security:** Linux has robust security features, including user permissions, access controls, and a strong emphasis on separating user space from the kernel.

- **Variety of Distributions:** There are numerous Linux distributions (distros), each catering to specific needs. Examples include Ubuntu, CentOS, Debian, and Arch Linux.

Common Use Cases:

- **Server Environments:** Many web servers, cloud servers, and enterprise servers run on Linux due to its stability and performance.

- **Embedded Systems:** Linux is widely used in embedded systems, including IoT devices.

- **Development Environments:** Linux is a preferred choice for developers due to its robust command-line interface and development tools.

Bash: It is a command processor that typically runs in a text window where the user types commands that cause actions. It's the default shell for many Linux distributions and earlier version of macOS.

Key Characteristics:

- **Scripting Language:** Bash is not just an interactive shell but also a scripting language. Users can write scripts to automate tasks, making it a powerful tool for system administration.

- **Command-Line Interface (CLI):** Bash provides a text-based interface where users can interact with the system by entering commands. This allows for efficient system management and scripting.

- **Job Control:** Bash allows users to manage processes, run background tasks, and switch between foreground and background jobs.

- **Variables and Control Structures:** Bash supports variables, loops, conditionals, and functions, providing a robust scripting environment.

- **Redirection and Pipelines:** Users can redirect input and output and create pipelines to chain commands, enabling powerful and flexible data manipulation.

Common Use Cases:

- **Automation:** Bash scripts are widely used for automating repetitive tasks and system administration.

- **System Configuration:** Bash is essential for configuring and managing various aspects of a Linux system.

- **Data Processing:** Bash, with its command-line tools, is used for text processing, data manipulation, and extraction.

5.3. Containerization and Orchestration

5.3.1. Containerization with Docker:

Docker is a comprehensive platform that revolutionizes the way applications are developed, shipped, and executed. It leverages containerization technology, allowing developers to encapsulate applications and their dependencies in lightweight, portable containers.

5.3.1.1. Key Concepts:

- **Docker Containers:** Containers are self-contained units that package an application and its dependencies. They ensure consistency across various environments, promoting seamless deployment and scalability.

- **Docker Images:** Docker images are the building blocks of containers. They serve as blueprints, containing all the necessary components for an application, including code, libraries, dependencies, and runtime.

- **Dockerfile:** Dockerfiles are scripts that define the steps for creating Docker images. Developers use Dockerfiles to specify the base image, application code, dependencies, and configuration.

- **Docker Registry:** Docker images are stored in registries, repositories that facilitate the sharing and distribution of images. Docker Hub is a popular public registry, and organizations often use private registries for security and control.

5.3.1.2. Use Cases:

Microservices Architecture: Docker is instrumental in implementing microservices architecture, allowing developers to containerize individual services, facilitating independent development, deployment, and scaling.

DevOps Practices: Docker is a cornerstone of DevOps practices, enabling the creation of reproducible environments. It plays a crucial role in CI/CD pipelines, ensuring consistency from development to production.

5.3.2. Container Orchestration with Kubernetes:

Kubernetes is an open-source container orchestration platform designed to automate the deployment, scaling, and management of containerized applications. It simplifies the complexities of deploying and managing containerized applications at scale.

5.3.2.1. Key Concepts:

- **Pods:** They are the smallest deployable units in Kubernetes, representing one or more containers that share network and storage resources. They are the basic building blocks for deploying applications.

- **ReplicaSets:** ReplicaSets ensure a specified number of replicas (identical copies) of a pod are running at all times. They are vital for achieving scalability and maintaining high availability.

- **Services:** Kubernetes Services enable communication and networking between different pods and external services. They provide a stable endpoint for accessing the application, regardless of the pod's underlying IP address.

- **Deployments:** Deployments are higher-level abstractions that manage ReplicaSets. They allow for updates, rollbacks, and ensure the desired state of the application, simplifying application lifecycle management.

- **ConfigMaps and Secrets:** ConfigMaps and Secrets are Kubernetes resources used for managing configuration data and sensitive information, respectively. They enhance security and configuration management.

5.3.2.2. Use Cases:

Scaling Applications: Kubernetes facilitates automatic scaling of applications based on demand through features like Horizontal Pod Autoscaling (HPA). This ensures optimal resource utilization and responsiveness.

High Availability: Kubernetes enhances the availability of applications by distributing workloads across multiple nodes and offering self-healing capabilities. This ensures uninterrupted service even in the face of failures.

5.3.3. Docker with Kubernetes:

Kubernetes seamlessly integrates with Docker, utilizing Docker containers as the fundamental deployment units. Developers specify Docker images in Kubernetes manifests, enabling a smooth transition from local development environments to scalable Kubernetes clusters. **While Docker excels at containerization,** Kubernetes focuses on orchestration. It automates the deployment, scaling, and management of Docker containers, providing a robust platform for running containerized applications at scale. Kubernetes ensures that the desired state of the application is maintained efficiently.

5.4. Provisioning Resources

5.4.1. CloudFormation:

It is a service provided by Amazon Web Services (AWS) that enables users to define and provision AWS infrastructure using a template-based approach. The service follows the Infrastructure as Code (IaC) paradigm, allowing developers to express infrastructure configurations as code.

5.4.1.1. Key Concepts:

- **CloudFormation Templates:** These are JSON or YAML files that describe the AWS resources needed for an application. Templates define the architecture and configuration of the infrastructure.

- **Stacks:** They are sets of AWS resources created and managed together. When you launch a CloudFormation stack, it provisions and configures the specified resources.

- **Resources:** The individual components defined in a CloudFormation template are resources, such as EC2 instances, S3 buckets, or databases. Each resource type corresponds to an AWS service.

- **Parameters and Outputs:** Parameters allow users to input custom values when creating or updating a stack. Outputs provide information about the resources created in a stack, making it easy to reference them in other stacks or applications.

5.4.1.2. Use Cases:

- **Infrastructure Automation:** CloudFormation enables the automation of infrastructure provisioning, making it easy to replicate and manage infrastructure as code.

- **Version Control:** Templates can be version-controlled, providing a history of changes and facilitating collaboration among development teams.

- **Stack Management:** Stacks allow for the management of related resources as a single unit, simplifying the creation, update, and deletion of infrastructure components.

5.4.2. Terraform:

Terraform is an open-source Infrastructure as Code (IaC) tool developed by HashiCorp. It supports multiple cloud providers, including AWS, Azure, Google Cloud, and various on-premises solutions. Terraform uses its own declarative configuration language.

5.4.2.1. Key Concepts:

- **Terraform Configuration Language:** Terraform uses a declarative configuration language to define infrastructure configurations. The language is designed to be human-readable and supports variables and modules.

- **Providers:** They are plugins that define and manage resources in a specific cloud or on-premises infrastructure. Each cloud provider is supported by a Terraform provider, allowing for a multi-cloud approach.

- **Resources and Modules:** Resources are the fundamental components of infrastructure, representing individual elements like virtual machines or storage. Modules are reusable collections of resources with defined inputs and outputs.

- **State Files:** Terraform maintains a state file that records the current state of the infrastructure. This file helps Terraform understand what changes are needed to achieve the desired configuration.

5.4.2.2. Use Cases:

- **Multi-Cloud Deployments:** Terraform's ability to support multiple cloud providers makes it suitable for organizations with a multi-cloud strategy. It provides a unified approach to managing resources across different platforms.

- **Infrastructure Versioning:** Terraform allows for version control of infrastructure configurations, providing a history of changes and facilitating collaboration. This ensures a clear audit trail of modifications.

- **Resource Composition:** Terraform's modular design allows users to compose complex infrastructure by combining and reusing modules. This promotes maintainability and scalability by encapsulating and abstracting infrastructure components.

5.4.3. Integration with Cloud Services:

- **CloudFormation:** It is specifically designed for AWS, offering deep integration with AWS services. It provides native support for AWS resources and seamless integration with other AWS management services.

- **Terraform:** It is cloud-agnostic and supports multiple cloud providers. This flexibility allows users to manage resources across different cloud platforms using a unified configuration language, making it a versatile tool for hybrid and multi-cloud scenarios.

5.4.4. Choosing Between CloudFormation and Terraform:

- **Cloud-Specific vs. Multi-Cloud:** Choose CloudFormation if you are working exclusively in AWS. Opt for Terraform if you need a multi-cloud solution to manage resources across different cloud providers.

- **Service Ecosystem:** Consider the specific AWS services and integrations you require. CloudFormation might be a more natural choice for AWS-centric projects due to its deep integration with AWS services.

- **Syntax Preferences:** Evaluate the syntax and language preferences of your team. Some teams may find the declarative syntax of CloudFormation more intuitive, while others may prefer Terraform's HCL (HashiCorp Configuration Language).

- Both **Cloud Formation** and **Terraform** provide powerful solutions for provisioning and managing infrastructure as code. The choice between them often depends on factors such as cloud provider preferences, multi-cloud requirements, and team familiarity with the respective tools. The ultimate goal is to select the tool that best aligns with the specific needs and preferences of your organization.

5.5. Automation and Resource Management with Ansible

Ansible is a robust open-source automation tool known for its simplicity, flexibility, and agentless architecture. It is designed to automate configuration management, application deployment, and other repetitive tasks, providing a streamlined approach to infrastructure management.

5.5.1. Key Concepts:

- **Playbooks:** They are written in YAML and define a set of tasks to be executed on target machines. They are the fundamental units for expressing Ansible automation.

- **Inventory:** Ansible uses an inventory file to list and organize target machines. This can be a static text file or

116

a dynamic inventory source, allowing flexibility in defining hosts.

- **Modules:** Ansible modules are small scripts that perform specific tasks on remote systems. Ansible includes a vast library of built-in modules for common operations, and users can create custom modules as needed.

- **Roles:** They provide a way to organize playbooks and share common configurations. They encapsulate tasks, handlers, variables, and other Ansible elements, promoting modular and reusable automation.

5.5.2. Use Cases:

Configuration Management: Ansible ensures consistent configurations across systems, automating tasks like package installation, file management, and system settings.

Application Deployment: It automates the deployment of applications, managing dependencies, and ensuring that applications run seamlessly across different environments.

Infrastructure as Code (IaC): Ansible allows users to define infrastructure as code, enabling the reproducible creation and configuration of infrastructure resources.

5.5.3. Key Features:

- **Agentless:** Ansible operates without the need for agent software on target machines. It communicates over SSH by default, making it lightweight and minimizing the maintenance overhead.

- **Idempotence:** Ansible playbooks and tasks are idempotent, meaning they can be run multiple times without changing the system's state. This ensures predictable and safe automation.

- **Extensibility:** Users can extend Ansible's functionality by creating custom modules, roles, and plugins. This allows Ansible to integrate with a wide range of systems and services.

- **Parallel Execution:** Ansible can execute tasks in parallel across multiple machines, optimizing performance and reducing the time required for automation processes.

5.5.4. Ansible Integration with Cloud and Infrastructure Services:

- Ansible has modules for major cloud providers (AWS, Azure, Google Cloud), enabling users to automate the provisioning and management of cloud resources.

- It is capable of managing network devices, making it a versatile tool for configuring and maintaining network infrastructure.

- It integrates with container orchestration tools (Docker, Kubernetes), providing automation for container deployment, configuration, and management.

5.6. Managed Services and their Role in Scalable Systems

Managed services play a crucial role in enabling scalable systems, providing organizations with the expertise and resources to effectively manage and adapt their IT infrastructure to meet evolving business demands. By outsourcing IT management tasks to managed service providers (MSPs), businesses can reap several benefits that contribute to scalability and overall success.

- **Enhanced Scalability and Flexibility:** Managed services help organizations scale their IT infrastructure seamlessly, adding or removing resources as needed to accommodate changing workloads and user demands. MSPs provide expertise in resource provisioning, cloud management, and infrastructure optimization, ensuring that systems can handle fluctuations in traffic and data volume without performance bottlenecks.

- **Cost-Efficiency and Optimization:** Managed services can significantly reduce IT costs by eliminating the need to hire, train, and maintain in-house IT staff. MSPs offer economies of scale, providing access to a pool of experienced IT professionals and shared infrastructure resources, which reduces the overall cost of IT operations.

- **Expertise and Proactive Management:** Managed services provide organizations with access to a team of experienced IT professionals who possess specialized knowledge and skills in various areas, including cloud computing, cybersecurity, and network management.

MSPs proactively monitor systems, identify potential issues, and implement preventative measures to minimize downtime and maximize uptime.

- **Improved Focus on Core Business:** By outsourcing IT management to MSPs, organizations can free up their internal IT teams to focus on strategic initiatives and core business functions. This allows businesses to concentrate on their areas of expertise and competitive advantage while ensuring that their IT infrastructure is well-managed and supports their business objectives.

- **Access to Latest Technologies and Trends:** Managed service providers stay at the forefront of emerging technologies and trends, providing organizations with access to the latest advancements in cloud computing, cybersecurity, and IT infrastructure. MSPs can help organizations adopt new technologies effectively, optimizing their IT environment for innovation and growth.

- **Reduced Risk and Improved Security:** Managed services help organizations mitigate security risks and enhance their cybersecurity posture. MSPs provide expertise in vulnerability assessments, intrusion detection, and incident response, ensuring that IT systems are protected from cyber threats and data breaches.

- **Compliance and Regulatory Support:** Managed services can assist organizations in complying with industry regulations and data privacy laws. MSPs have experience in navigating complex compliance requirements and implementing appropriate controls to protect sensitive data.

- **Continuous Improvement and Innovation:** Managed services promote continuous improvement and innovation within IT environments. MSPs regularly evaluate and optimize IT systems, identify areas for enhancement, and implement new technologies to improve performance, efficiency, and security.

CHAPTER 6

SCALING

CHAPTER 6:

SCALING

In the dynamic realm of technology and digital innovation, the success of any product is often measured not just by its initial impact but by its ability to adapt and thrive in the face of increasing demands and user interactions. This chapter explores the critical concept of "Scaling" – an imperative aspect often underestimated in the development lifecycle but paramount for sustained success.

Why dedicate an entire chapter to Scaling? The answer lies in the inherent challenge that arises as a product gains popularity and usage. A failure to anticipate and address scaling issues can lead to disastrous consequences, ranging from sluggish performance to complete system failures. It's not merely about adding more servers; it's about understanding the nuanced landscape of scaling and optimizing systems for high traffic and data loads.

A common pitfall lies in neglecting scaling considerations during the initial stages of product development. Many products falter not because of inherent flaws in their core design but due to a lack of foresight regarding the surge in demand. As user numbers grow, an unprepared system can buckle under the pressure, resulting in a frustrating user experience and potential business losses.

Scaling is a multifaceted challenge, extending far beyond the simple act of adding more servers. Horizontal scaling, vertical scaling, database optimization, caching strategies, Content Delivery Networks (CDNs), and selecting the right architectural framework – these are the pillars upon which a scalable system stands. Each aspect represents a critical element in the overall structure, and overlooking any one of these can pose a risk to the integrity of the entire system.

Another common misstep is oscillating between extremes – either building a system that is too simplistic to handle scaling challenges or overengineering a complex architecture that becomes difficult to manage. Striking the right balance is an art. The foundation should be simple, yet robust, with the innate capacity to expand seamlessly as demands grow.

6.1. Introduction: Importance of Scalability

Scalability has become a critical factor for the success of any system, whether it's a business application, a website, or a network infrastructure. Scalability refers to the ability of a system to handle growing amounts of work, or its potential to be enlarged to accommodate that growth. It is a fundamental consideration in designing and managing modern systems to ensure they can meet the increasing demands of users, data, and transactions.

Scalability in Modern Systems

It encompasses various aspects depending on the context of the system. In software and application development, it could mean the ability to handle an increasing number of users or requests without compromising performance. For hardware or infrastructure, scalability might involve the ability to expand computational resources, storage capacity, or network bandwidth seamlessly.

There are generally two types of scalability:

1. **Vertical Scalability (Scaling Up):** This involves adding more resources, such as upgrading to a more powerful server with increased CPU, RAM, or storage capacity.

2. **Horizontal Scalability (Scaling Out):** This involves adding more instances of resources, such as adding more servers to distribute the workload and enhance performance.

6.2. Why Scalability Matters

6.2.1. Business Perspective:

- **Meeting Growing Demand:** Scalability is crucial for businesses experiencing growth. It ensures that as the user base, data load, or transaction volume increases, the system can seamlessly adapt to meet the demand without degradation in performance.

- **Enhancing User Experience:** A scalable system ensures a consistent and reliable user experience. It prevents issues such as slow response times, downtime, or errors that could negatively impact user satisfaction and loyalty.

- **Cost-Efficiency:** Scalability allows businesses to optimize costs. Instead of investing in a large infrastructure upfront, resources can be added incrementally as needed, reducing initial expenses and improving financial flexibility.

6.2.2. Technical Perspective:

- **Performance Optimization:** Scalability is directly linked to performance optimization. By distributing the workload across multiple resources, systems can handle more concurrent users and provide faster response times, ensuring efficient operation even during peak loads.

- **Fault Tolerance:** Scalable systems are often designed with redundancy and failover mechanisms. This enhances reliability and ensures that if one component fails, the system can still operate without significant disruption.

- **Future-Proofing:** Technology is dynamic, and system requirements evolve. Scalability future-proofs systems, allowing them to adapt to changing needs and incorporate new technologies without requiring a complete overhaul.

Scalability is a cornerstone for modern systems, offering both business advantages in terms of growth and cost-efficiency, and technical benefits related to performance, reliability, and adaptability. Organizations that prioritize scalability are better positioned to navigate the challenges of a dynamic and expanding digital landscape.

6.3. Core Principles of Scalable Design

The core principles which make the system more scalable are:

- **Modularity and Decoupling:** Break down the system into modular components with well-defined interfaces.

126

This allows for independent development, deployment, and scaling of individual modules, promoting flexibility and ease of maintenance.

- **Load Balancing:** Distribute incoming network traffic or workload across multiple servers to prevent any single server from becoming a bottleneck. Load balancing ensures optimal resource utilization and helps in achieving horizontal scalability.

- **API-First Design:** API-first design treats APIs as the primary interface for interacting with the system. This approach promotes loose coupling and enables easier integration with external systems or third-party applications.

- **Elasticity:** Design systems to be elastic, allowing them to dynamically scale resources up or down based on demand. This involves automated provisioning and de-provisioning of resources to handle varying workloads efficiently.

- **Horizontal Scaling:** Prioritize the ability to scale out by adding more instances or nodes rather than scaling up by upgrading existing resources. This approach enhances fault tolerance, provides better resource utilization, and supports incremental growth.

- **Statelessness:** Keep components stateless whenever possible. Statelessness simplifies scaling since any instance of a stateless component can handle any request, making it easier to distribute the workload across multiple instances.

- **Caching Strategies:** Implement effective caching mechanisms to reduce the load on backend resources. Caching frequently accessed data or computation results can significantly improve response times and overall system performance.

- **Database Scaling Techniques:** Choose appropriate database scaling techniques, such as sharding (horizontal partitioning of data) or replication, to handle increased data loads. Consider NoSQL databases for flexible and scalable data storage.

- **Asynchronous Communication:** Utilize asynchronous communication patterns, such as message queues or event-driven architectures, to decouple components and enable efficient handling of background tasks, promoting scalability and responsiveness.

6.3.1. Scalability vs. Performance: Understanding the Distinction

- **Scalability:** Refers to a system's ability to handle a growing amount of work or its potential to accommodate increased demand by adding resources. Scalability is about the system's capacity to grow and manage a larger load effectively.

- **Performance:** Encompasses the responsiveness, speed, and efficiency of a system under a specific workload. While scalability aims for effective growth, performance focuses on optimizing the system's current capabilities.

Scalability and performance are related but distinct concepts. A system can be highly performant but not scalable if it struggles when the workload surpasses a certain threshold. Conversely, a scalable system may not exhibit high performance if its resources are not efficiently utilized.

6.3.2. Strategies for Scalable Design

The strategies for scalable design are:

- **Modular Architecture:** Break down the system into independent modules with well-defined interfaces to facilitate independent development, testing, and scaling.

- **Microservices Approach:** Divide the system into smaller, self-contained services that can be scaled and deployed independently. This promotes loose coupling and reduces dependency management complexity.

- **Data Partitioning:** Partition large datasets across multiple servers to distribute storage and processing load, improving performance and scalability.

- **Caching Strategies:** Implement caching mechanisms to store frequently accessed data in memory, reducing database load and improving response times.

- **Load Balancing:** Distribute incoming traffic across multiple servers to prevent overloading individual nodes and ensure efficient resource utilization.

- **Content Delivery Networks (CDNs):** Utilize CDNs to cache and deliver static content, such as images and videos, from geographically dispersed servers, reducing latency and improving global accessibility.

- **Automated Provisioning:** Automate the process of provisioning and configuring new resources to quickly adapt to changing demand.

- **Cloud-Based Infrastructure:** Leverage cloud-based infrastructure to dynamically provision and scale resources based on real-time demand, offering flexibility and cost-efficiency.

By incorporating these foundational concepts and strategies into the design process, software architects can create systems that are not only capable of handling increasing demands but also maintain performance, resilience, and cost-effectiveness.

6.4. Critical Elements Influencing Scalability

6.4.1. Infrastructure: On-premise vs. Cloud vs. Hybrid Solutions

The choice of infrastructure, whether on-premise, cloud, or hybrid, plays a crucial role in determining the scalability of an application or system. Each option presents distinct advantages and limitations, making the selection process a critical consideration for organizations seeking to scale effectively.

- **On-premise Infrastructure**

On-premise infrastructure, where hardware and software are housed within an organization's own physical premises, offers the highest degree of control and security. This approach is ideal for organizations with stringent data privacy requirements or those who prefer to manage their IT infrastructure directly. However, on-premise infrastructure can be costly to maintain and scale, especially as workloads grow.

- **Cloud Infrastructure**

Cloud infrastructure, such as Amazon Web Services (AWS), Microsoft Azure, or Google Cloud Platform (GCP), provides a scalable and cost-effective solution for handling fluctuating workloads. Cloud services offer on-demand access to computing resources, allowing organizations to provision and scale resources as needed without significant upfront investments in hardware and software. However, cloud-based infrastructure can be less secure and may raise concerns about data privacy and control.

- **Hybrid Infrastructure**

Hybrid infrastructure combines the benefits of both on-premise and cloud environments. Organizations can maintain sensitive data and critical applications on-premise while leveraging cloud services for less sensitive workloads that require elasticity and scalability. This approach offers a balance of control, security, and scalability, but it also increases the complexity of managing two distinct IT environments.

Scaling

Here's a table summarizing the key considerations for each infrastructure type:

Factor	On-premise	Cloud	Hybrid
Cost	High upfront investment, ongoing maintenance costs	Lower upfront investment, pay-as-you-go model	Varies depending on the split between on-premise and cloud
Performance	Dedicated hardware, full control over optimization	Scalable resources, can handle bursts in demand	Can optimize on-premise for performance-critical workloads and cloud for scalability
Security	Full control over physical security and data access	Cloud security depends on provider's policies and practices	Requires careful consideration of security between on-premise and cloud environments
Control	Full control over hardware and software	Limited control over underlying infrastructure	Varies depending on the split between on-premise and cloud

The choice of infrastructure depends on the specific needs and priorities of your organization. If you require high levels of control and security, on-premise infrastructure may be the best option. If you need scalability and flexibility at a lower upfront cost, cloud infrastructure may be a better choice. And if you need a balance of control, security, and scalability, a hybrid infrastructure may be the best solution.

It's important to carefully evaluate your organization's requirements and consider the trade-offs between each infrastructure type before making a decision.

6.4.2. Database Scalability: Sharding, Replication, and Partitioning

Database scalability is a critical consideration in designing and managing large-scale systems to handle growing amounts of data and increasing user loads.**Sharding, replication**, and **partitioning** are **three common techniques** employed **to achieve scalability in databases**.

- **Sharding**

Sharding is a technique employed in database scalability where data is horizontally partitioned across multiple independent databases or shards. Each shard operates as a self-contained unit, holding a distinct subset of the overall dataset. The distribution of data among shards is typically based on specific criteria, such as ranges of values or hash functions. Sharding offers a scalable solution as it allows the system to distribute the workload across different servers, preventing a single server from becoming a bottleneck. This approach enhances both the storage capacity and the processing capabilities of the database.

- **Replication**

Replication involves the creation and maintenance of copies, or replicas, of a database on multiple servers. In a replicated setup, changes made to one copy, known as the master, are mirrored or propagated to other copies, referred to as slaves. This not only provides a level of fault tolerance but also enhances read performance. By distributing read operations across replicas, the overall system can handle a higher volume of read requests, contributing to improved efficiency. Replication is a valuable technique for ensuring high availability and data redundancy in database systems.

- **Partitioning**

Partitioning is a strategy that entails dividing a large database table into smaller, more manageable pieces known as partitions. These partitions are created based on specific criteria, such as ranges of values, lists, or hash functions. Each partition operates as a distinct entity, and data within a partition is typically related. This technique improves query performance by allowing the database system to scan only relevant partitions rather than the entire dataset. Moreover, partitioning facilitates easier management of data, including tasks such as backup, recovery, and maintenance. It is particularly effective in scenarios where certain subsets of data are accessed or updated frequently.

These three techniques—**sharding**, **replication**, and **partitioning**—are often utilized in combination to address different aspects of scalability, fault tolerance, and performance optimization within large-scale database systems. The choice of which technique or combination to use depends on the specific requirements and characteristics of the application and its data.

6.4.3. Stateful vs. Stateless Design

The terms "**stateful**" and "**stateless**" are often used in the context of software architecture, particularly when discussing web applications. The distinction between these two approaches lies in how they manage and maintain application state.

Stateful applications keep track of and maintain information about the user's current session or state. This information is typically stored on the server, and each subsequent request from the user includes a unique identifier that allows the server to associate the request with the corresponding user session. Examples of stateful applications include shopping carts, online banking platforms, and social media applications.

Stateless applications, on the other hand, do not maintain any state information on the server. Each request is treated independently, and all necessary information must be included in the request itself. This approach simplifies the application architecture and makes it more scalable, as servers can handle requests without relying on persistent state information. Examples of stateless applications include RESTful APIs and content delivery networks (CDNs).

Key Differences between Stateful and Stateless Design

Here's a table summarizing the key differences between stateful and stateless design:

Feature	Stateful Design	Stateless Design
State Maintenance	Server maintains user session state	No persistent state maintained
Request Dependency	Subsequent requests rely on previous state information	Each request is self-contained
Scalability	Scalability challenges due to state management	Highly scalable due to stateless nature
Complexity	More complex architecture due to state management	Simpler architecture due to lack of state management
Resilience	More prone to failures if state is not replicated	Less susceptible to failures due to lack of state

Choosing between Stateful and Stateless Design

The choice between stateful and stateless design depends on the specific requirements of the application. If the application requires maintaining user sessions or tracking user interactions, a stateful approach may be necessary. However, if the application is performance-critical and needs to be highly scalable, a stateless approach is often preferred.

Considerations for Choosing Stateful Design:

- **User sessions:** Applications that need to maintain user sessions, such as shopping carts or online banking platforms, require stateful design.

- **User preferences:** Applications that need to store user preferences or settings, such as personalized news feeds or language settings, may benefit from stateful design.

- **Real-time interactions:** Applications that require real-time interactions, such as chat applications or collaborative editing tools, may also need stateful design.

Considerations for Choosing Stateless Design:

- **Performance:** Applications that require high performance and scalability, such as RESTful APIs or content delivery networks (CDNs), often benefit from stateless design.

- **Simplicity:** Applications with simpler requirements and fewer dependencies may be easier to develop and maintain using stateless design.

- **Resilience:** Stateless applications are generally more resilient to failures, as they do not rely on persistent state information.

The choice between **stateful** and **stateless** design depends on the specific needs and priorities of the application. Carefully evaluate your application's requirements and consider the trade-offs between each approach before making a decision.

6.4.4. Concurrency and Parallelism: Maximizing Resource Utilization

Concurrency and parallelism are two fundamental concepts in computing that play a crucial role in maximizing resource utilization and achieving efficient performance. While they are often used interchangeably, there is a subtle distinction between the two.

Concurrency refers to the ability of a system to handle multiple tasks or requests simultaneously. It creates the illusion of parallelism by interleaving the execution of multiple tasks, allowing them to share the same resources, such as CPU cores or memory. This technique is particularly useful for interactive applications where responsiveness is critical.

Parallelism, on the other hand, is the actual execution of multiple tasks or instructions simultaneously using multiple processing resources. This can be achieved through hardware parallelism, such as multi-core processors or GPUs, or through software parallelism, such as using threads or processes. Parallelism is essential for computationally intensive tasks that can benefit from the combined processing power of multiple resources.

Benefits of Concurrency and Parallelism

Concurrency and parallelism offer several benefits for modern computing systems:

- **Improved responsiveness:** By interleaving tasks, concurrency can improve the responsiveness of an application, especially for user interactions.

- **Enhanced throughput:** Parallelism can significantly increase the throughput of an application by distributing work across multiple processing units.

- **Resource utilization:** Both concurrency and parallelism can improve resource utilization by allowing multiple tasks to share the same resources more efficiently.

- **Scalability:** Concurrent and parallel applications can be scaled to handle increasing workloads by adding more processing resources.

Trade-offs of Concurrency and Parallelism

While concurrency and parallelism offer significant advantages, they also introduce certain trade-offs:

- **Complexity:** Implementing and managing concurrent and parallel applications can be more complex due to the need to synchronize task execution and handle potential race conditions.

- **Overhead:** The overhead associated with task scheduling and synchronization can reduce the overall performance benefits.

- **Debugging:** Debugging concurrent and parallel applications can be more challenging due to the non-deterministic nature of their execution.

6.5. Architectural Patterns for Scalability

Architectural patterns provide a blueprint for designing and building software systems that are scalable, resilient, and maintainable. Three key architectural patterns that address scalability challenges are microservices architecture, event-driven architecture, and load balancing strategies.

6.5.1. Microservices Architecture: Isolating Responsibilities

Microservices architecture is a software development approach that structures an application as a suite of small, independent services. Each microservice is responsible for a specific business capability and is self-contained, meaning it has its own data store, logic, and network communication.

Benefits of Microservices Architecture for Scalability:

- **Independent scalability:** Microservices can be scaled independently, allowing you to scale up or down individual services without affecting the entire system.

- **Fault isolation:** Failures in one microservice do not cascade to the entire system, limiting the impact of failures and enhancing overall resilience.

- **Technology heterogeneity:** Microservices can be developed using different programming languages and technologies, enabling the use of the best tools for each task.

6.5.2. Event-Driven Architecture: Asynchronous Communication and Processing

Event-driven architecture (EDA) is a software design pattern that relies on asynchronous communication between loosely coupled components. Events are messages that represent state changes or occurrences in the system, and they are exchanged between components using message brokers or queues.

Benefits of Event-Driven Architecture for Scalability:

- **Asynchronous processing:** Events can be processed asynchronously, decoupling the producer and consumer of events and allowing for efficient handling of bursts in traffic.

- **Decoupling:** Components communicate through events, reducing interdependencies and enabling independent scaling and development.

- **Resilience:** Event-driven systems are inherently resilient, as events can be stored and processed even if some components are unavailable.

6.5.3. Load Balancing Strategies: Distributing Client Requests Efficiently

Load balancing refers to the technique of distributing client requests across multiple servers or resources to optimize resource utilization and improve responsiveness. Load balancers act as intermediaries between clients and servers, routing requests to the most suitable server based on various factors, such as server load, performance, and location.

Common Load Balancing Strategies:

- **Round robin:** Requests are distributed to servers in a cyclical manner, ensuring that each server receives an equal share of requests.
- **Least connections:** Requests are routed to the server with the fewest active connections to balance the load and prevent overloading.
- **Weighted round robin:** Servers are assigned weights based on their capacity, and requests are distributed accordingly, directing more traffic to servers with higher capacity.
- **Content-based routing:** Requests are routed to servers based on the content of the request, such as the requested URL or user-specific data.
- **Geolocation-based routing:** Requests are routed to servers based on the user's location, ensuring optimal response times and minimizing latency.

Choosing the Right Architectural Patterns for Scalability

The choice of architectural patterns for scalability depends on the specific requirements and characteristics of the application. **Microservices architecture** is particularly well-suited for complex applications with evolving requirements, while **event-driven architecture** is beneficial for applications with high throughput and asynchronous processing needs. **Load balancing** strategies are essential for distributing traffic and optimizing resource utilization, regardless of the chosen architectural pattern.

6.6. Scaling Strategies: Vertical and Horizontal

6.6.1. Vertical Scaling: When and How to Scale Up

Vertical scaling, also known as scaling up, involves increasing the processing power and storage capacity of a single server or instance. This approach is typically employed when the application's resource requirements are relatively predictable and can be met by upgrading the hardware of the existing infrastructure.

When to Use Vertical Scaling:

- **Predictable resource requirements:** If the application's resource needs are relatively consistent and can be accurately predicted, vertical scaling is a straightforward and cost-effective approach.

- **Limited traffic fluctuations:** For applications with minimal traffic spikes or sudden surges in demand, vertical scaling can provide sufficient resources without the complexity of managing multiple servers.

- **Legacy applications:** In cases where the application is tightly coupled with the underlying hardware or requires specialized hardware configurations, vertical scaling may be the only viable option.

How to Implement Vertical Scaling:

- **Upgrade hardware:** Increase the CPU cores, RAM, and storage capacity of the existing server or instance to handle the growing resource demands.

- **Optimize software:** Optimize the application code and configuration to minimize resource utilization and improve performance.

- **Monitor performance:** Continuously monitor the system's performance metrics, such as CPU usage, memory consumption, and response times, to ensure adequate resources and identify potential bottlenecks.

6.6.2. Horizontal Scaling: When and How to Scale Out

Horizontal scaling, also known as scaling out, involves adding more servers or instances to the infrastructure to distribute the workload across multiple resources. This approach is particularly effective for applications with unpredictable traffic patterns and high scalability requirements.

When to Use Horizontal Scaling:

- **Unpredictable traffic:** For applications with fluctuating traffic demands, horizontal scaling provides the flexibility to add or remove servers as needed, accommodating spikes and troughs in traffic.

- **High scalability:** If the application needs to handle increasing workloads and user demands, horizontal scaling allows for seamless expansion of the infrastructure without disrupting service.

- **Cost-efficiency:** Horizontal scaling can be more cost-effective than vertical scaling, especially for long-term usage, as it distributes the load across multiple lower-cost servers.

How to Implement Horizontal Scaling:

- **Load balancing:** Implement a load balancer to distribute incoming requests across multiple servers, ensuring optimal resource utilization and preventing overloading.

- **Auto-scaling:** Utilize auto-scaling mechanisms to automatically add or remove servers based on predefined performance metrics or traffic patterns.

- **Data replication:** Implement data replication strategies to ensure data consistency and availability across multiple servers.

6.6.3. Auto-scaling: Automated Decision-making for Resource Allocation

Auto-scaling is a dynamic resource management technique that automatically scales up or down the application infrastructure based on real-time performance metrics and traffic patterns. This approach eliminates the need for manual intervention and ensures that the infrastructure adapts to changing demands, optimizing resource utilization and maintaining service levels.

Benefits of Auto-scaling: It comes with tons of benefits, some of are:

- **Cost-effectiveness:** Auto-scaling optimizes resource allocation, reducing costs by provisioning resources only when needed.

- **Responsiveness:** Auto-scaling responds to changes in demand in real-time, ensuring that the infrastructure

145

can handle spikes in traffic without compromising performance.

- **Simplified management:** Auto-scaling simplifies infrastructure management by automating resource provisioning and scaling decisions.

- **Improved resilience:** Auto-scaling can help prevent service disruptions by automatically adding or removing servers in response to failures or performance bottlenecks.

Implementing Auto-scaling: Implementation of auto scaling can be done by using following things:

- **Define scaling policies:** Establish policies that define when and how to scale up or down, considering performance metrics, traffic patterns, and cost constraints.

- **Choose auto-scaling tools:** Utilize cloud-based auto-scaling services or implement open-source auto-scaling solutions.

- **Monitor resource utilization:** Continuously monitor resource utilization and performance metrics to optimize scaling policies and ensure effective resource allocation.

6.7. Code and Query Optimization

Code Optimization: The process of improving the efficiency of a program's code to enhance its performance.

Techniques:

- Use efficient algorithms and data structures.

- Minimize unnecessary loops and function calls.

- Optimize resource utilization, such as memory and CPU usage.

- Utilize compiler optimizations and coding best practices.

Query Optimization: Improving the efficiency of database queries to reduce response times.

Techniques:

- Properly index database columns to speed up query execution.

- Optimize SQL queries for better performance.

- Organize data to minimize redundancy and improve query efficiency.

- Analyze and optimize execution plans.

6.7.1. Caching Strategies: Reducing Database Load

Caching involves storing frequently accessed data in a temporary storage to reduce the need to fetch it from the original source.

Cache Aside: In the Cache Aside, the cache consistency depends on the application itself. Because the cache doesn't sit on the top of the data store. Whenever data is requested application first checks into the cache and returns the data if exists, otherwise the application goes directly to the data store to get the data and then it stores that thing in the cache for future use and returns the data to the client.

Application manages cache consistency. Less efficient for writes, but good for simple scenarios.

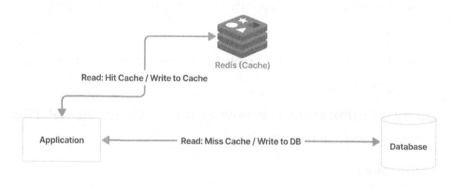

Cache-Aside Strategy

Inline Cache: Inline Cache is a strategy in which cache consistency is dependent on the cache. Because the cache sits directly on the data store and the data store is accessed through the cache. Whenever data is requested, the application looks directly into the cache and returns the data if it exists, otherwise, the cache would go to the data store to get the data and return it to the cache, then the cache will remember it for the future use and returns the data. Whenever again the same data is requested it is returned from the cache.

Cache manages consistency. More efficient for writes, but adds complexity.

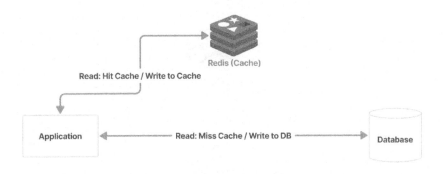

Cache-Aside Strategy

Write-Through: It comes from the Inline cache strategy in which the cache consistency depends on the cache itself. The write-Through cache is that whenever data is requested, it goes directly to the cache and would return it if it exists. Otherwise, the cache goes directly to the data store to get the data, then the cache will remember it for future use and return it to the client.

But whenever data is updated, it directly goes to the cache to update it, and then the cache updates it into the data store then the data is returned to the client. Which leads to very good cache consistency.

Write updates both cache and data store simultaneously. High consistency, but less performant.

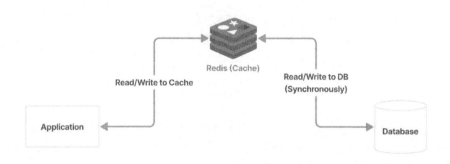

Write-Through Cache Strategy

Write-Behind: There is an issue with the Write-through cache strategy from where the Write-behind cache strategy comes into play.In the Write-Through cache strategy, the data is written first in the cache, and then the cache stores it in the underlying data store. This is when the writing process completes.

But In the Write-behind cache strategy, the data is stored just in the cache and the data write process is completed and returned. The cache behind itself handles storing the data in the data store asynchronously.

This is what makes the Write-behind cache strategy better than the Write-Through cache strategy.Write updates cache first, then data store asynchronously. High performance, but risks data loss in case of crash.

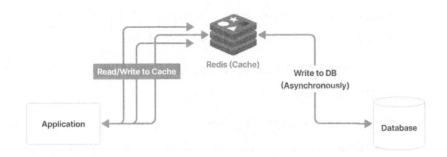

Write-Behind Cache Strategy

Comparisons:

- **Cache Aside vs. Inline Cache:** Cache Aside is easier to implement but requires more application logic for consistency. Inline Cache is more efficient for writes but requires additional infrastructure.

- **Write-Through vs. Write-Behind:** Write-Through offers higher data consistency but can be slower due to synchronous writes. Write-Behind offers better performance but risks data loss if the cache fails before writing to the data store.

It all depends on the needs of your system and which strategy is fit for it.

6.7.2. Content Delivery Networks (CDNs): Improving User Experience

CDNs are distributed networks of servers that deliver web content, including HTML pages, JavaScript files, stylesheets, images, and videos, to users based on their geographic locations.

Techniques:

- **Content Distribution:** Distribute copies of static content across multiple servers globally.

- **Caching:** CDNs cache content close to the end-users, reducing latency.

- **Load Balancing:** Distribute incoming traffic across multiple CDN servers to ensure optimal performance and reliability.

- **Security Features:** Many CDNs provide security features such as DDoS protection and Web Application Firewalls (WAFs).

Utilizing a **Content Delivery Network (CDN)** ensures faster content delivery by serving data from servers in close geographic proximity to users, leading to improved website performance and reduced load on the origin server.

6.8. Practical Case Studies: Scalability in Action

Scalability is a critical concern for businesses of all sizes, from startups to established enterprises. As demand grows, so does the need to handle increased traffic and workload efficiently. In this article, we will explore real-world scenarios of scaling challenges and the solutions that companies have implemented to overcome them. We will also share lessons learned from industry giants that can be applied to your own business.

6.8.1. Real-world Scenarios of Scaling Challenges and Solutions:

Netflix - Scaling Video Streaming:

- **Challenge:** Netflix had to find a way to deliver video streaming to millions of users around the world without experiencing buffering or outages.

- **Solution:** Netflix built its own content delivery network (CDN) that uses a geographically distributed network of servers to deliver content closer to users. This reduced latency and improved streaming quality.

Amazon - Managing Peak Season Demand:

- **Challenge:** Amazon had to find a way to handle the huge influx of orders during peak season without compromising its delivery times.

- **Solution:** Amazon invested in automation and robotics to improve its fulfillment process. It also built a network of fulfillment centers around the world to get products closer to customers.

Google - Handling Search Queries:

- **Challenge:** Google had to find a way to process billions of search queries per day and return relevant results in milliseconds.

- **Solution:** Google developed a massive data center infrastructure and built its own search engine algorithms that can rank billions of web pages.

Uber - Scaling On-Demand Transportation:

- **Challenge:** Uber had to find a way to connect drivers and riders in real time and manage a dynamic transportation network.

- **Solution:** Uber developed a mobile app that uses GPS technology to track drivers and riders. It also built a complex algorithms to optimize pricing and dispatch drivers efficiently.

6.8.2. Lessons Learned from Industry Giants on Scaling

By observing how industry giants have tackled scalability challenges, we can glean valuable insights that can be applied to businesses of all sizes. Here are some key lessons learned:

1. Embrace Continuous Innovation: Industry giants like Amazon, Google, and Facebook are constantly innovating their technology and processes to stay ahead of the curve. This allows them to scale efficiently and adapt to changing market conditions.

Lesson: Invest in research and development, foster a culture of experimentation, and be open to adopting new technologies.

2. Build a Scalable Infrastructure: Investing in a reliable and scalable infrastructure is crucial for accommodating growth. This includes cloud-based solutions, geographically distributed data centers, and distributed computing architectures.

Lesson: Choose technologies that are designed to scale horizontally and avoid vendor lock-in.

3. Automate and Optimize: Automating repetitive tasks and optimizing workflows can significantly improve efficiency and speed up scaling efforts. This frees up human resources for more strategic activities.

Lesson: Identify tasks that can be automated and leverage tools like machine learning and AI to optimize processes.

4. Prioritize Data-driven Decision Making: Collecting and analyzing data allows companies to make informed decisions about scaling initiatives. This helps them identify bottlenecks, measure the effectiveness of different solutions, and track progress over time.

Lesson: Invest in data analytics tools and build a culture of data-driven decision making.

5. Foster a Culture of Agility and Adaptability: The ability to quickly adapt to changing market conditions and unforeseen challenges is vital for sustainable growth. This requires a culture that encourages agility, collaboration, and rapid iteration.

Lesson: Encourage risk-taking, empower employees to make decisions, and create a culture that learns from failures.

6. Build Strong Partnerships: Collaborating with strategic partners can accelerate scaling efforts and provide access to expertise, resources, and new markets.

Lesson: Identify potential partners that share your vision and values, and build mutually beneficial relationships.

7. Focus on Customer Experience: Scaling successfully should never come at the expense of customer experience. Maintaining a focus on customer satisfaction and delivering exceptional value will drive long-term loyalty and growth.

Lesson: Invest in customer experience initiatives, gather feedback regularly, and continuously improve your offerings based on customer needs.

6.9. Conclusion: Building a Scalability Mindset

In today's rapidly evolving business landscape, the ability to scale effectively is no longer a luxury, but a necessity. By embracing the lessons learned from industry giants and implementing the scalability essentials outlined in this document, you can position your business for long-term success.

Here's a recap of the key takeaways:

1. Cultivating a Culture of Continuous Improvement:

- Foster a growth mindset that encourages experimentation, learning, and adaptation.

- Invest in research and development to stay ahead of the curve with innovative technologies.

- Encourage data-driven decision making and use metrics to track progress and identify areas for improvement.

2. Staying Informed: Resources for Ongoing Learning:

- Attend industry conferences and workshops to learn from experts and network with peers.

- Subscribe to relevant publications and blogs to stay updated on the latest trends in scalability.

- Utilize online resources and courses to deepen your understanding of specific technologies and methodologies.

By consistently learning and adapting, you can develop a strong scalability mindset that will guide you through the challenges and opportunities of growth. Remember, scalability is not a destination, but a continuous journey. Embrace the process, learn from your experiences, and never stop striving for improvement.

CHAPTER 7

MONITORING

CHAPTER 7:

MONITORING

As systems grow in complexity, identifying errors and pinpointing areas of slow responsiveness becomes a formidable challenge. A scenario may arise where a system functions optimally in one region but experiences delays in another, illustrating the necessity of a robust monitoring strategy. Without comprehensive monitoring, the intricacies of runtime bugs and performance issues, influenced by factors such as region, device, and operating system, remain elusive.

Monitoring becomes essential in unfolding system errors with detailed context, expediting the debugging and resolution process. In an era where systems continually expand in scale and complexity, debugging without the aid of monitoring becomes a challenging task. Furthermore, the absence of monitoring leaves developers unaware of the challenges faced by end-users, as testing cannot foresee all potential issues.

This chapter offers an exhaustive examination of various aspects, from the significance of network monitoring in system architecture to real-time monitoring and analytics. Illustrated with appropriate strategies, tools, and case studies, it enriches the understanding of monitoring network services, assuring up-to-the-minute view of system performance.

The section further dives into performance and infrastructure monitoring nuances, exploring strategies, tools, and methodologies for tracking resource utilization. Considering the scalability and visibility challenges, maintaining an efficient monitoring infrastructure becomes crucial.

159

The realms of security and compliance monitoring unfold next, emphasizing innovative methods and the fine balance between security and performance. The chapter also covers techniques for business transaction and availability monitoring to foster operational efficiency and risk reduction.

Resource monitoring and capacity planning strategies take the spotlight next, focusing on predictive analytics utilization for resource allocation. It addresses the complexities of resource monitoring, ensuring long-term stability and adaptability.

Wrapping up, the chapter digresses towards Application Performance Monitoring (APM), presenting challenges, potential solutions, and proven practices. Real-world case studies highlight how APM conflicts were successfully resolved.

This chapter will help in understanding, implementing, and refining the practice of monitoring in system architecture. Traversing through APM and system monitoring nuances, we aim to provide the necessary tools and knowledge to build enduring, high-performing digital ecosystems.

7.1. Application Performance Monitoring (APM)

7.1.1. Definition and Scope of APM in System Architecture

Application Performance Monitoring (APM) is a set of tools and practices used to monitor the performance, health, and behavior of an application and its underlying infrastructure. It helps identify and diagnose performance issues, optimize resource utilization, and ensure a positive user experience.

Scope: APM encompasses various aspects of an application, including:

- **Application code:** Monitoring code execution times, resource consumption, and errors.

- **Application infrastructure:** Monitoring servers, databases, networks, and other components.

- **User experience:** Monitoring response times, page load times, and other metrics that impact user interaction.

Role in System Architecture: APM sits alongside other monitoring tools within the system architecture, providing vital insights into the application's behavior and performance. It interacts with various systems, including:

- **System monitoring tools:** Sharing data and cooperating with tools that monitor infrastructure components such as servers, networks, and storage.

- **Application logging systems:** Collecting and analyzing log files for detailed information about application events and errors.

- **Alerting and notification systems:** Triggering alerts based on pre-defined thresholds to notify IT teams about potential issues.

7.1.2. The Three Core Data Types in APM:

These are quantitative measurements that provide a snapshot of application performance at specific points in time.

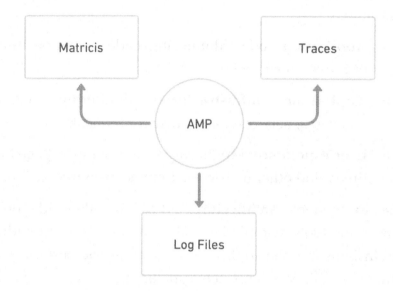

Metrics: Metrics are quantitative measurements that provide a high-level view of the performance and health of an application. Examples include response time, CPU usage, memory utilization, and error rates. Metrics offer a quick way to identify trends and anomalies.

Traces: Traces provide a detailed, transaction-centric view of the application's performance. A trace follows the journey of a specific transaction as it traverses different components of the application. This helps identify bottlenecks and dependencies in the system.

Log Files: Log files contain detailed information about events and activities within an application. They are valuable for troubleshooting and debugging. APM tools analyze log data to identify issues and correlate them with other performance metrics.

7.1.3. How APM Integrates with Overall System Monitoring:

APM integrates with overall system monitoring in several ways:

- **Data sharing:** APM tools share data with other monitoring tools to provide a comprehensive view of system performance. This allows for correlation and identification of complex issues that involve multiple components.

- **Alerting and event correlation:** APM tools can trigger alerts based on specific events and performance metrics. These alerts can be correlated with alerts from other monitoring tools to identify root causes and expedite troubleshooting.

- **Unified dashboards and reports:** APM tools provide dashboards and reports that integrate data from various sources, including application performance, system metrics, and log files. This provides a unified view of system health and performance.

Benefits of APM Integration:

- Improved visibility into overall system performance.

- Faster identification and resolution of performance issues.

- Reduced mean time to repair (MTTR) and downtime.

- Proactive identification and prevention of potential problems.

- Improved operational efficiency and resource utilization.

- Enhanced user experience and satisfaction.

7.2. Advanced APM Techniques and Tools

In recent years, APM has evolved beyond traditional monitoring techniques to incorporate advanced technologies like AI and ML and leverage the scalability and flexibility of cloud-based solutions.

7.2.1. AI and ML in APM:

AI (Artificial Intelligence) and ML (Machine Learning) have become integral components of advanced APM solutions, providing enhanced capabilities for monitoring, analysis, and predictive insights. Here's an in-depth discussion on their roles in APM:

Automatic anomaly detection: ML algorithms can analyze vast amounts of data to automatically identify anomalous behavior and potential issues, even before they impact performance.

Predictive analysis: AI can be used to predict future performance bottlenecks and resource constraints, allowing for proactive resource management and scaling.

Root cause analysis: ML can analyze traces and logs to identify the root cause of performance issues, significantly reducing the time and effort required for troubleshooting.

User behavior analysis: AI can be used to analyze user behavior data and identify patterns that can be used to optimize the application for better user experience.

Automated performance optimization: AI can automate tasks such as code optimization and resource allocation to improve performance and resource utilization.

7.2.2. Cloud-Based APM Solutions and Integration:

Cloud-based APM solutions leverage the scalability and flexibility of cloud infrastructure to enhance monitoring capabilities. Key aspects include:

Scalability: Cloud-based APM solutions can scale horizontally to accommodate growing application workloads and the increasing complexity of distributed systems. They can handle monitoring for applications deployed across multiple cloud environments.

Cost-effectiveness: Cloud-based solutions eliminate the need for upfront investment in hardware and infrastructure.

Distributed Tracing: Cloud APM tools often offer distributed tracing capabilities, allowing organizations to trace transactions across microservices and distributed architectures. This is crucial for understanding performance bottlenecks in modern, cloud-native applications.

Integration with Cloud Services: Cloud APM solutions seamlessly integrate with various cloud services, such as AWS CloudWatch, Azure Monitor, or Google Cloud Monitoring. This integration provides a unified view of both application and infrastructure metrics.

Container and Orchestration Support: Cloud APM tools are designed to monitor applications running in containers and orchestrated environments like Kubernetes. They provide insights into container performance, resource utilization, and orchestration-related metrics.

Integrating cloud-based APM into system architecture:

- **Data collection:** Cloud-based APM solutions collect data from application components deployed across different cloud environments.

- **Data aggregation and analysis:** The collected data is aggregated and analyzed in the cloud platform, using AI and ML algorithms.

- **Visualization and reporting:** Cloud-based dashboards and reports provide insights into application performance, resource utilization, and user behavior.

- **Alerting and notification:** Cloud-based solutions can trigger alerts and notifications based on pre-defined thresholds and performance trends.

7.2.3. Examination of Specific APM Tools - Dotcom-Monitor:

Dotcom-Monitor is an APM tool that focuses on website and web application monitoring. Key features include:

Synthetic monitoring: The tool supports synthetic monitoring to simulate user interactions and test application performance under controlled conditions. This is valuable for proactive testing and identifying potential issues before they impact real users.

Real user monitoring (RUM): Captures real-time user behavior data to identify performance bottlenecks and optimize user experience.

Application tracing: Tracks individual transactions to pinpoint performance issues and identify root causes.

Load Testing: Dotcom-Monitor offers load testing capabilities to simulate heavy traffic conditions and assess how an application performs under stress. This is essential for capacity planning and identifying potential performance bottlenecks.

7.3. Monitoring Network Services

7.3.1. Importance of Network Monitoring in System Architecture:

Network monitoring plays a crucial role in maintaining a healthy and reliable system architecture. It offers several benefits, including:

- **Early detection of network issues:** Identifying and resolving network problems quickly before they significantly impact application performance and user experience.

- **Improved network performance:** Optimizing network resources and identifying bottlenecks to ensure smooth and efficient data flow.

- **Enhanced security:** Detecting suspicious activity and potential security threats on the network.

- **Increased uptime and availability:** Proactive maintenance and troubleshooting help minimize downtime and ensure continuous operation of critical network services.

- **Reduced costs:** Timely identification and resolution of issues can prevent costly network outages and data loss.

By implementing effective network monitoring, organizations can gain a comprehensive understanding of their network activity, identify potential problems proactively, and ensure a stable and reliable environment for their applications and users.

7.3.2. Strategies for Monitoring Network Services:

Several strategies can be employed for effective network service monitoring:

- **Ping:** This basic tool checks the network connectivity to a specific host and measures its response time.

- **Traceroute:** This tool identifies the path taken by data packets across the network, helping diagnose routing issues and identify bottlenecks.

- **SNMP (Simple Network Management Protocol):** This protocol allows monitoring devices to gather data from network components like routers and switches, providing information on performance metrics, errors, and utilization.

- **Netflow and IPFIX:** These protocols provide detailed information about network traffic flow, enabling identification of traffic patterns, anomalies, and security threats.

- **Port monitoring:** This strategy monitors specific network ports used by services like DNS, FTP, SMTP, POP3, and IMAP, ensuring their availability and responsiveness.

- **Application-specific probes:** These tools simulate user interactions with specific network services, measuring their performance and identifying potential problems.

7.3.3. Utilization of Tools like Dotcom-Monitor for Network Service Monitoring:

Dotcom-Monitor offers various features for comprehensive network service monitoring:

- **Synthetic monitoring:** Simulates user interactions with network services like DNS, FTP, SMTP, POP3, and IMAP, measuring response times and identifying performance bottlenecks.

- **Real user monitoring (RUM):** Captures real-time user data on network service performance, providing insights into their experience across different locations and devices.

- **API monitoring:** Monitors the performance and availability of RESTful APIs, ensuring smooth data exchange between applications.

- **Multi-step transactions:** Simulates complex workflows involving multiple network services, identifying performance issues across the entire chain.

- **Global monitoring network:** Deploys monitoring agents across various locations around the world, providing insights into geographically diverse network performance.

- **Alerting and notification:** Triggers real-time alerts based on pre-defined thresholds and performance metrics, notifying IT teams of potential problems.

- **Reporting and analytics:** Provides detailed reports and dashboards for analyzing network performance trends and identifying areas for improvement.

Benefits of using Dotcom-Monitor:

- Covers various network services and protocols.

- Provides immediate visibility into network performance and potential issues.

- Ensures consistent performance across different locations.

- Reduces manual effort and ensures timely identification of problems.

- Adapts to the needs of your growing network and infrastructure.

By leveraging tools like Dotcom-Monitor, organizations can gain comprehensive insights into their network service performance, identify and resolve issues quickly, and ensure a reliable and robust network infrastructure.

7.4. Real-Time Monitoring and Analytics

Real-time data and its analysis have become critical for organizations to thrive. Real-time monitoring and analytics provide a continuous stream of insights into system performance, user behavior, and market trends, enabling immediate action and informed decision-making.

7.4.1. The Need for Real-Time Monitoring in System Architecture

Traditional monitoring approaches, relying on batch processing and periodic reports, are no longer sufficient. They lack the immediacy and granularity needed to respond to dynamic environments and identify issues quickly. Real-time monitoring offers several advantages:

- Real-time data allows for immediate identification of anomalies and potential problems, preventing them from escalating and impacting performance.

- Having access to real-time insights empowers faster and more informed decisions based on current information, leading to better outcomes.

- Monitoring user behavior in real-time allows for identifying and mitigating issues impacting user experience, leading to increased satisfaction.

- Continuously analyzing system performance in real-time helps identify resource bottlenecks and optimize resource utilization, resulting in improved efficiency and cost savings.

- Real-time monitoring enables proactive detection of security threats and potential failures, allowing for quicker response and improved system resilience.

7.4.2. Tools and Techniques for Implementing Real-Time Data Analytics

Several tools and techniques are available for implementing real-time data analytics:

Data Acquisition:

- **Streaming APIs:** Platforms like Twitter and Kafka provide streaming APIs to access real-time data feeds.

- **IoT Sensors:** Sensors embedded in devices and machines continuously generate data that needs real-time analysis.

- **Log Management Systems:** Centralized log management systems collect and analyze application and system logs in real-time.

Data Processing:

- **Stream Processing Engines:** Apache Spark Streaming and Apache Flink are popular tools for processing high-volume data streams in real-time.

- **In-Memory Databases:** Databases like Redis and Memcached provide high performance for storing and retrieving real-time data.

- **Real-Time Analytics Platforms:** Platforms like Splunk and Datadog offer dashboards and visualizations for analyzing real-time data.

Analysis and Visualization:

- **Real-Time Dashboards:** Real-time dashboards provide visual representations of key performance indicators

(KPIs) and metrics, allowing for immediate identification of trends and anomalies.

- **Alerting and Notification Systems:** These systems trigger alerts based on pre-defined thresholds, notifying stakeholders of potential issues.

- **Machine Learning:** Machine learning algorithms can be applied to real-time data to detect patterns, predict future trends, and automate decision-making.

The choice of tools and techniques depends on various factors, including the volume and velocity of data, the desired level of complexity, and the specific use case.

7.4.3. Case Studies Demonstrating the Impact of Real-Time Monitoring

Real-time monitoring and analytics have led to significant improvements across various industries. Big tech companies are at the forefront of utilizing real-time monitoring and analytics to gain valuable insights, optimize their services, and improve user experience. Here are a few case studies showcasing the impact:

1. Netflix:

- **Use case:** Real-time monitoring of video streaming performance to identify and address buffering issues before users experience them.

- **Impact:** Reduced buffering rates by 20%, leading to a significantly improved user experience and increased customer satisfaction.

- **Technology:** Netflix uses a combination of tools, including Dynatrace and Splunk, to monitor various aspects of its streaming infrastructure, including server performance, network latency, and video encoding quality.

2. Amazon:

- **Use case:** Real-time monitoring of inventory levels and customer demand to optimize product placement and fulfillment processes.

- **Impact:** Reduced out-of-stock situations by 15% and improved delivery times by 10%, leading to increased customer satisfaction and revenue growth.

- **Technology:** Amazon relies on a massive data infrastructure based on Apache Spark and other real-time processing technologies to analyze vast amounts of data from inventory systems, customer orders, and delivery logistics.

3. Google:

- **Use case:** Real-time monitoring of website traffic and user behavior to personalize search results and ad campaigns.

- **Impact:** Increased click-through rates on ads by 25% and improved the relevance of search results for users, leading to a more engaging online experience.

- **Technology:** Google utilizes its own internal real-time data processing platform, along with various machine learning algorithms, to analyze user behavior and personalize its services.

7.5. Performance and Infrastructure Monitoring

Monitoring system performance and infrastructure is crucial for ensuring the smooth operation of IT environments. Effective monitoring helps identify bottlenecks, troubleshoot issues, and optimize resource utilization. Here are strategies, tools, and methods for monitoring performance and infrastructure:

7.5.1. Strategies for Monitoring System Performance and Infrastructure

Effective performance and infrastructure monitoring requires a comprehensive strategy encompassing various aspects:

Metrics Collection:

- **Identify key performance indicators (KPIs):** Define metrics that reflect system health, user experience, and resource utilization. Examples include CPU utilization, response time, memory usage, disk I/O, and network traffic.

- **Establish baselines:** Determine ideal performance levels for each metric based on historical data and expected workloads.

- **Collect data at appropriate intervals:** The frequency of data collection depends on the volatility of the system and desired level of detail.

Data Analysis:

- **Identify trends and anomalies:** Analyze collected data to detect unusual fluctuations and potential performance bottlenecks.

- **Correlate metrics:** Analyze relationships between different metrics to identify root causes of performance issues.

- **Set alerts and notifications:** Configure alerts to inform stakeholders about critical events or deviations from established baselines.

Actionable Insights:

- **Prioritize issues:** Analyze the severity and impact of identified issues to determine the order of resolution.

- **Troubleshoot and diagnose problems:** Utilize diagnostic tools and log analysis to pinpoint the root cause of performance bottlenecks.

- **Implement corrective actions:** Apply appropriate solutions to address performance problems and improve system health.

7.5.2. Tools and Methods for Tracking Resource Utilization

Several tools and methods are available for tracking resource utilization:

Operating System Tools:

- **Built-in performance monitoring tools:** Most operating systems offer utilities like Task Manager (Windows) and Activity Monitor (macOS) for basic resource utilization monitoring.
- **Performance counters:** Operating systems expose performance counters that provide detailed information about CPU, memory, disk, and network activity.

Agent-Based Monitoring Tools:

- **Dedicated monitoring solutions:** Tools like ELK Stack, Nagios, Zabbix, and Datadog provide comprehensive performance monitoring capabilities, including resource utilization tracking, alerting, and visualization.
- **Cloud monitoring services:** Cloud providers like AWS, Azure, and Google Cloud offer built-in monitoring services for resources provisioned within their platforms.

Open-Source Monitoring Tools:

- **Prometheus:** An open-source monitoring system that collects and stores metrics from various sources, including infrastructure and applications.
- **Grafana:** An open-source dashboarding tool for visualizing and analyzing metric data collected by Prometheus and other sources.

7.5.3. Addressing Challenges in Scalability and Visibility

As systems and infrastructure scale, monitoring complexity increases. Here are strategies to address scalability and visibility challenges:

Distributed Monitoring:

- Utilize distributed monitoring architectures with agents deployed across various servers and network devices.

- Implement data aggregation and consolidation to provide a centralized view of performance data.

Cloud-Based Monitoring:

- Leverage cloud-based monitoring solutions that offer scalability and centralized data management.

- Utilize containerization technologies like Docker and Kubernetes to easily deploy and manage monitoring agents.

Automated Monitoring and Alerting:

- Automate routine monitoring tasks to reduce manual effort and improve efficiency.

- Configure intelligent alerts based on predefined thresholds and anomaly detection algorithms.

Visualization and Reporting:

- Implement dashboards and reports to visualize resource utilization trends and identify potential issues.

- Utilize interactive dashboards for real-time analysis and exploration of performance data.

Collaboration and Communication:

- Establish clear communication channels for reporting performance issues and coordinating resolution efforts.

- Utilize collaboration tools to share insights and facilitate problem-solving across teams.

7.6. Security and Compliance Monitoring

7.6.1. Advanced Methodologies in Security Monitoring:

Traditional security monitoring relying on signature-based detection is no longer sufficient to address today's evolving threat landscape. Advanced methodologies are necessary to defend against sophisticated cyberattacks.

Here are some advanced methodologies in security monitoring:

- **Threat Intelligence:** Integrating threat intelligence feeds into monitoring systems provides real-time insights into emerging threats and vulnerabilities.

- **Security Information and Event Management (SIEM):** These platforms collect and analyze logs and events from various sources to identify suspicious activities and potential security incidents.

- **User and Entity Behavior Analytics (UEBA):** This technology utilizes machine learning to analyze user behavior patterns and identify anomalies that might indicate malicious activity.

- **Network Traffic Analysis (NTA):** NTA tools analyze network traffic patterns and identify unusual activity that might be indicative of lateral movement or data exfiltration.

- **Endpoint Detection and Response (EDR):** EDR solutions provide real-time visibility into endpoint activities and enable rapid detection and response to threats.

- **Security Orchestration, Automation, and Response (SOAR):** SOAR platforms automate repetitive tasks associated with security incident response, streamlining the process and improving efficiency.

- **Machine Learning and AI:** Utilize machine learning algorithms and artificial intelligence to analyze large datasets and identify complex security threats, reducing false positives and improving the efficiency of threat detection.

7.6.2. Monitoring for Compliance in System Architecture:

Monitoring the system for architectural compliance helps to quickly detect in- consistencies between the intended behavior and its actual implementation. Compliance monitoring ensures adherence to industry regulations and data privacy laws. It involves:

- Identifying relevant regulations and compliance requirements.

- Mapping compliance requirements to specific system controls and processes.

- Implementing monitoring solutions to track and audit system activity relevant to compliance.

- Generating reports and logs to demonstrate compliance with regulations.

Integrating compliance monitoring into system architecture requires:

- Defining clear roles and responsibilities for compliance monitoring.

- Establishing automated workflows for gathering and analyzing compliance-related data.

- Utilizing tools and platforms specifically designed for compliance monitoring.

- Regularly reviewing and updating compliance monitoring strategies.

7.6.3. Balancing Security and Performance in Monitoring Strategies:

Excessive monitoring can negatively impact system performance. Finding the right balance between security and performance is crucial for optimal system operation.

Here are strategies for balancing security and performance:

- **Prioritize monitoring based on risk:** Focus on monitoring critical systems and processes with the highest risk profile.

- **Optimize monitoring agent configurations:** Minimize resource utilization of monitoring agents to avoid performance bottlenecks.

- **Utilize cloud-based monitoring solutions:** Cloud-based solutions offer scalability and can help reduce the performance impact on monitored systems.

- **Implement tiered monitoring:** Utilize different monitoring levels for different systems based on their criticality and performance requirements.

- **Leverage automation:** Automate routine monitoring tasks to minimize manual overhead and resource consumption.

- **Utilize machine learning:** Machine learning algorithms can be used to identify anomalous behavior and prioritize alerts, reducing the need for constant monitoring.

7.7. Business Transaction and Availability Monitoring

Monitoring business transactions and ensuring high availability and uptime of systems are crucial aspects of managing an organization's IT infrastructure. These practices help enhance operational efficiency, reduce risks, and ensure that critical business processes run smoothly. Here are some key considerations for both business transaction monitoring and availability monitoring:

7.7.1. Monitoring business transactions for operational efficiency and risk mitigation.

Business transaction monitoring focuses on tracking and analyzing the flow of information through essential business processes. This involves:

- **Identifying key business transactions:** Define critical transactions that impact business goals, customer experience, and revenue generation.

- **Map transaction flow:** Trace the journey of each transaction across various systems and infrastructure components.

- **Monitor transaction performance:** Track key metrics like response time, success rate, and error rate for each transaction.

- **Identify bottlenecks and performance issues:** Analyze transaction data to identify slowdowns, outages, and potential points of failure.

- **Correlate transaction data with other metrics:** Analyze transaction data alongside system metrics like CPU, memory, and network utilization to pin down root causes of performance issues.

By monitoring business transactions, organizations can:

- Identify and address bottlenecks that hinder transaction processing speed.

- Proactively identify and mitigate potential failures that could disrupt business operations.

- Monitor compliance-related business transactions to ensure adherence to regulations.

- Identify and resolve issues that impact customer experience during key transactions.

7.7.2. Techniques for Ensuring High Availability and Uptime of Systems:

High availability (HA) ensures continuous operation of critical systems and minimizes downtime. Several techniques can be used to achieve HA:

- **Redundancy:** Implement redundant components for critical systems like servers, storage, and network connections. This minimizes the impact of single points of failure.

- **Disaster Recovery (DR):** Develop a comprehensive DR plan to recover from major outages or disasters. This includes regular backups, offsite data storage, and failover capabilities.

- **Load Balancing:** Distribute workload across multiple servers to prevent overloading and ensure responsiveness.

- **Autoscaling:** Automatically scale resources up or down based on demand to optimize resource utilization and maintain performance.

- **Monitoring and alerting:** Implement comprehensive monitoring systems to identify potential issues and trigger alerts for immediate response.

- **Proactive maintenance:** Perform regular maintenance tasks and updates to prevent system failures.

7.8. Resource Monitoring and Capacity Planning:

7.8.1. Long-term Strategies for Resource Monitoring and Capacity Planning:

Long-term resource monitoring and capacity planning involve assessing the current and future needs of an IT infrastructure to ensure that it can support the organization's growth. It includes monitoring resource usage over extended periods and making informed decisions about infrastructure expansion or optimization.

Key Components:

- **Historical Data Analysis:** Regularly analyze historical performance data to identify trends and patterns in resource usage.

- **Demand Forecasting:** Use business projections and trends to forecast future resource demands accurately.

- **Scenario Planning:** Plan for different scenarios, considering factors such as seasonal variations, new product launches, or anticipated changes in user behavior.

7.8.2. Implementing Predictive Analytics in Resource Allocation:

Predictive analytics involves using historical data, statistical algorithms, and machine learning techniques to identify the likelihood of future outcomes. In resource allocation, predictive analytics can help anticipate future resource needs and optimize allocation accordingly.

Key Components:

- **Machine Learning Models:** Develop models that analyze patterns in resource usage to predict future demands.

- **Dynamic Adjustment:** Implement systems that dynamically adjust resource allocation based on real-time predictions.

- **Anomaly Detection:** Utilize predictive analytics to detect anomalies or unexpected events that might impact resource requirements.

7.8.3. Addressing the Complexities of Resource Monitoring:

Resource monitoring can be complex due to diverse technologies, distributed systems, and dynamic workloads. Addressing these complexities involves implementing robust monitoring solutions and strategies.

Key Components:

- **Comprehensive Monitoring Tools:** Invest in tools that provide visibility into all aspects of the IT infrastructure, including servers, networks, databases, and applications.

- **Cross-Platform Compatibility:** Ensure that monitoring solutions can seamlessly integrate with different platforms and technologies.

- **Scalability:** Choose monitoring tools that can scale with the growing size and complexity of the infrastructure.

7.9. Challenges and Solutions in APM

7.9.1. Common Challenges in Application Monitoring

Efficient monitoring is vital for ensuring optimal performance. However, common challenges such as scalability issues, high costs, and the complexity of diverse data and cloud environments often impede seamless application monitoring. Let's explore these obstacles and their implications for organizations striving to maintain peak application performance.

- **Scalability:** Modern applications are increasingly complex and dynamic, with many microservices and containers. Traditional APM tools may struggle to scale with the increasing volume and velocity of data generated by these applications. This can lead to performance issues and inaccurate insights.

- **Cost:** Traditional APM solutions can be expensive to purchase, implement, and maintain. Additionally, the cost of scaling these solutions to handle larger applications can be significant.

- **Data Complexity:** APM tools collect a vast amount of data from various sources, making it difficult to analyze and identify relevant insights. Traditional tools often lack the capabilities to handle this complexity.

- **Cloud Complexity:** Many applications today are deployed in hybrid or multi-cloud environments. Monitoring performance across these different environments can be challenging with traditional tools that haven't kept pace with cloud technology.

- **Lack of Visibility:** Traditional APM tools often focus on specific components of an application, lacking a holistic view of the entire application ecosystem. This can make it difficult to identify root causes of performance issues.

- **Alert Fatigue:** Traditional APM tools generate a large number of alerts, many of which are irrelevant or false positives. This can lead to alert fatigue, making it difficult for IT teams to identify and respond to critical issues.

7.9.2. Solutions and Best Practices to Address These Challenges

Addressing challenges in application monitoring necessitates strategic solutions. We will into best practices, such as adopting modern APM tools and implementing efficient data management, to optimize performance and enhance overall monitoring effectiveness.

Modern APM Solutions: Choose modern APM solutions designed for scalability and cloud-native applications. These solutions use distributed tracing, AI/ML for root cause analysis, and real-time monitoring to provide comprehensive insights into application performance.

Data Management: Implement robust data management practices to ensure efficient data collection, storage, and retrieval. Leverage technologies like data lakes and data warehouses to manage large volumes of data.

Cloud-Native APM: Utilize cloud-native APM solutions designed to integrate seamlessly with public clouds and handle the dynamic nature of cloud environments.

Holistic Monitoring: Choose APM solutions that provide a holistic view of the entire application ecosystem, including application components, infrastructure, and user experience.

Alert Optimization: Implement intelligent alerting systems that filter out irrelevant alerts and prioritize critical issues. Use AI/ML to identify patterns and predict potential issues before they occur.

Cost Optimization: Utilize cost-effective APM solutions that offer flexible pricing models and pay-as-you-go options.

Consider cloud-based APM solutions that eliminate the need for upfront hardware investments.

7.9.3. Case studies on overcoming APM barriers

Here are three case studies on how big tech companies overcame APM barriers using modern solutions and best practices:

Case Study 1: Google Cloud - Managing Complexity with Distributed Tracing

Challenge: Google Cloud's platform consists of numerous microservices, generating massive amounts of data. Traditional APM tools struggled to handle the data volume and lacked visibility into microservice interactions.

Solution: Google Cloud implemented a distributed tracing system based on OpenTelemetry. This enabled them to trace requests across microservices, identify bottlenecks, and optimize performance.

Results: Google Cloud achieved significant performance improvements and reduced troubleshooting time by 50%. They were also able to identify and resolve issues faster, leading to improved customer experience.

Case Study 2: Netflix - Leveraging AI for Root Cause Analysis

Challenge: Netflix's streaming platform experiences dynamic traffic patterns, making it difficult to pinpoint performance issues. Traditional APM tools struggled to keep up and provided limited insights.

Solution: Netflix developed its own AI-powered APM system called Chaos Monkey. This system actively introduces controlled failures to identify weak points in the platform and simulate real-world scenarios.

Results: Netflix achieved a 5x reduction in mean time to resolution (MTTR) and significantly improved platform stability. They were also able to proactively identify and address potential issues before they impacted users.

Case Study 3: Amazon Web Services (AWS) - Embracing Cloud-Native APM

Challenge: AWS offers a vast range of cloud services, making it challenging to monitor performance across different environments with traditional tools. These tools also lacked the agility and scalability needed for a rapidly evolving cloud platform.

Solution: AWS developed its own cloud-native APM solution called Amazon CloudWatch. This solution integrates seamlessly with other AWS services and provides a comprehensive view of performance across the entire cloud environment.

Results: AWS achieved improved visibility into its complex cloud infrastructure and reduced troubleshooting time. They were also able to scale their monitoring capabilities to meet the demands of their growing platform.

CHAPTER 8

BIG DATA & ANALYTICS

CHAPTER 8:

BIG DATA & ANALYTICS

In the ever-evolving landscape of technology, the role of Big Data and Analytics has become a cornerstone in designing scalable systems. This chapter highlights the significance of these elements and their critical role in the modern digital ecosystem.

The challenge of handling large volumes of data is a common stumbling block for many expansive systems. Initially, systems may not be prepared to manage the sheer scale of data, leading to slow responses or even system failures. The journey from merely coping with data to effectively utilizing it is pivotal. Big Data isn't just about storage; it's about turning vast, complex datasets into actionable insights.

Modern giants in the tech industry, such as Meta and Amazon, exemplify the power of Big Data. They analyze user activities and preferences, tailoring content and recommendations to individual interests. This strategic use of data not only enhances user engagement but also drives business objectives, such as increased session times and sales.

In this chapter, we will explore the essentials of Big Data and Analytics, focusing on its role in scalable system design. We'll start with an overview of Big Data, its evolution, and the challenges it presents. The discussion will then shift to the key components of data analysis solutions, including data collection, storage, processing, and visualization. We'll also look at how Big Data analytics drives competitive advantages across various sectors and examine different types of analytics. The chapter concludes with an overview of the tools and technologies that are pivotal in Big Data analytics, providing a clear and concise understanding of this complex field.

8.1. Introduction to Big Data & Analytics

8.1.1. Overview of Big Data and Data Analytics

Big data simply refers to extremely large data sets. This size, combined with the complexity and evolving nature of these data sets, has enabled them to surpass the capabilities of traditional data management tools. This way, data warehouses, and data lakes have emerged as the go-to solutions to handle big data, far surpassing the power of traditional databases.

Data Analytics is the process of analyzing data in order to extract meaningful data from a given data set. These analytics techniques and methods are carried out on big data in most cases, though they certainly can be applied to any data set.

Big Data Analytics combines the power of advanced analytics with the vast amounts of data in order to extract valuable insights, make predictions, and optimize processes. It encompasses various analytical techniques, including descriptive analytics, diagnostic analytics, predictive analytics, and prescriptive analytics.

8.1.2. The Evolution and Challenges of Big Data:

The concept of Big Data has evolved over the years, driven by technological advancements and the increasing digitization of information. Traditionally, data processing involved structured data in manageable volumes. The rise of big data is driven by several factors:

- **Technological advancements:** Increased computing power, cheaper storage solutions, and the development of new data processing frameworks like Hadoop and Spark.

- **Growth of the internet and digital devices:** The proliferation of sensors, social media platforms, and online transactions has led to an exponential increase in data generation.

- **Data-driven decision making:** Companies and organizations are increasingly realizing the value of using data to make informed decisions.

8.1.3. Understanding the Characteristics of Big Data

Big data is defined by its unique characteristics, which differentiate it from traditional data. Due to the increasing volume, velocity, variety, veracity, and value of data, some data management challenges cannot be solved with traditional database and processing solutions. That's where data analysis solutions come in.

A brief definition of the five challenges will help you understand each one before you move on.

1. Volume

Volume means the amount of data that will be ingested by the solution — the total size of the data coming in. Solutions must work efficiently across distributed systems and be easily expandable in order to accommodate spikes in traffic.

2. Velocity

Velocity means the speed of data entering a solution. Many organizations now require near real-time ingestion and processing of data. The high velocity of data results in a shorter time to analyze than traditional data processing can provide. Solutions must be able to manage this velocity efficiently. Processing systems must be able to return results within an acceptable time frame.

3. Variety

Data can come from many different sources. Variety means the number of different sources and the types of sources — that the solution will use. Solutions need to be sophisticated enough to manage all the different types of data while providing accurate analysis of the data

4. Veracity

Veracity is the degree to which data is accurate, precise, and trusted. It is contingent on the integrity and trustworthiness of the data. Solutions should be able to identify the common flaws in the data and fix them before the data is stored. This is known as data cleansing.

5. Value

Value is the ability of a solution to extract meaningful information from the data that has been stored and analyzed. Solutions must be able to produce the right form of analytical results to inform business decision-makers and stakeholders of insights using trusted reports and dashboards.

8.2. Components of a Data Analysis Solution

8.2.1. Ingest/Collect: Strategies for Data Collection:

The first step in a data analysis solution is to ingest or collect data. Strategies for data collection include:

- **Batch Processing:** Collecting and processing data in predefined, periodic intervals. This is suitable for scenarios where real-time processing is not critical.

- **Real-time Streaming:** Ingesting and processing data as it is generated, allowing for real-time insights. This is crucial for applications requiring immediate responses, such as IoT and financial trading.

- **Data Connectors:** Implementing connectors to various data sources, such as databases, APIs, sensors, and logs, to gather data from diverse origins.

- **Data Integration:** Combining data from multiple sources to create a unified and comprehensive dataset.

8.2.2. Store: Secure and Scalable Storage Solutions

The collected data needs to be stored efficiently and securely. Popular storage solutions for big data include:

- **Hadoop Distributed File System (HDFS):** A scalable and fault-tolerant distributed file system designed for big data.

- **Cloud storage services:** Amazon S3, Microsoft Azure Blob Storage, and Google Cloud Storage offer scalable and cost-effective cloud-based storage solutions.

- **NoSQL databases:** Designed for unstructured and semi-structured data, these databases offer flexibility and scalability.

- **Data warehouses:** Traditional data warehouses provide structured storage for historical data and support complex data analysis queries.

The choice of storage solution depends on factors like data size, access requirements, performance needs, and budget constraints.

8.2.3. Process/Analyze: Data Processing and Analysis Techniques

This stage involves transforming and analyzing the stored data to extract meaningful insights. Common techniques include:

- **Data cleaning and preprocessing:** Removing errors, inconsistencies, and irrelevant information from the data.

- **Data transformation:** Converting data into a format suitable for analysis.

- Data mining: Applying statistical and machine learning algorithms to discover patterns and trends.

- **Data visualization:** Creating charts, graphs, and other visual representations to communicate insights effectively.

8.2.4. Consume/Visualize: Data Querying and BI Tools

This stage allows users to access and interact with the analyzed data. Tools and techniques include:

- **Data querying languages:** SQL and NoSQL query languages enable users to retrieve specific data subsets based on their needs.

- **Business intelligence (BI) tools:** Platforms like Tableau, Power BI, or Looker for creating interactive and visually appealing dashboards and reports.

- **Data storytelling:** Presenting data insights in a compelling and engaging way to drive decision-makin

- **Data Visualization:** Using charts, graphs, and other visual elements to represent complex data in an easily understandable format.

By integrating these components seamlessly, organizations can create a comprehensive data analysis solution that supports the entire data lifecycle, from collection to visualization, enabling informed decision-making and driving business success.

8.3. Planning and Implementing Data Analysis Solutions

8.3.1. Identifying Data Sources and Their Implications

The first step in planning a data analysis solution is to identify relevant data sources. It involves:

- **Understanding business goals and objectives:** What are the key questions that need to be answered? What insights are needed to improve decision-making?
- **Identifying potential data sources:** Internal databases, external databases, sensor data, social media data, web scraping, etc.
- **Evaluating data quality and accessibility:** Assessing the accuracy, completeness, and consistency of the data. Identifying any legal or ethical concerns regarding data collection and use.
- **Understanding data formats and structures:** Structured, semi-structured, or unstructured data?
- **Estimating data volume and velocity:** How much data needs to be collected and processed? How quickly is the data generated?

8.3.2. Evaluating Processing Solutions and Their Fit

Once data sources are identified, appropriate processing solutions need to be chosen. This involves:

- **Considering the characteristics of the data:** Volume, velocity, variety, veracity, and value.

- **Evaluating available technologies and frameworks:** Hadoop, Spark, NoSQL databases, cloud storage services, etc.

- **Analyzing costs and resources:** Hardware, software, personnel, and maintenance costs.

- **Choosing the right tools for data ingestion, storage, processing, and analysis:** Data pipelines, ETL tools, data mining algorithms, visualization platforms, etc.

- **Ensuring scalability and performance:** The solution should be able to handle growing data volumes and deliver timely insights.

8.3.3. Learning from Data: Analytics and Optimization

Data analysis is an iterative process. Once the data is processed, it needs to be analyzed and interpreted to extract valuable insights. This involves:

- **Applying appropriate analytics techniques:** Statistical analysis, machine learning, deep learning, etc.

- **Developing data models and visualizations:** Representing the data in a way that facilitates understanding and interpretation.

- **Discovering patterns and trends:** Identifying significant relationships and correlations in the data.

- **Communicating insights and driving action:** Presenting findings in a clear and compelling way to stakeholders.

- **Optimizing processes and decision-making:** Using data-driven insights to improve efficiency, reduce costs, and gain competitive advantage.

- **Continuously learning and iterating:** As new data is collected and analyzed, the data analysis solution should be updated and refined to ensure its continued relevance and effectiveness.

Planning and implementing a successful data analysis solution requires careful consideration of various factors, from identifying relevant data sources to choosing the right processing technologies and applying appropriate analytics techniques. By continuously learning from the data and iteratively refining the solution, organizations can unlock the full potential of their data and make smarter decisions.

8.4. The Competitive Edge of Big Data

8.4.1. How Big Data Analytics Drives Competitive Advantage

In today's data-driven economy, businesses that can leverage big data effectively have a significant competitive advantage. Here are some key ways big data analytics helps businesses gain an edge:

1. Improved decision-making: By analyzing large volumes of data, businesses can identify trends, patterns, and correlations that would be difficult or impossible to see with traditional methods. This data-driven approach leads to better-informed decisions across all areas of the organization, from marketing and sales to product development and operations.

2. Enhanced customer experience: Big data allows businesses to personalize the customer experience by understanding individual needs and preferences. This can be done through analyzing customer behavior data, social media interactions, and purchase history. By providing relevant and targeted offers and recommendations, businesses can foster loyalty and increase customer satisfaction.

3. Innovation and new product development: Big data analysis can help businesses identify new market opportunities and develop innovative products and services that meet the evolving needs of customers. By analyzing market trends, competitor activity, and customer feedback, businesses can stay ahead of the curve and bring new offerings to market faster.

4. Increased operational efficiency: Big data analytics can be used to optimize operations and improve efficiency across the organization. By analyzing data on production processes, supply chains, and resource utilization, businesses can identify areas for improvement and implement changes to optimize efficiency and reduce costs.

5. Risk management and fraud detection: Big data analytics can help businesses identify and mitigate risks by analyzing data on past events, customer behavior, and financial transactions. By identifying patterns and anomalies, businesses can proactively detect and prevent fraud, cyberattacks, and other potential issues.

8.4.2. Accenture Report on Big Data and Business Outcomes

A study by Accenture titled **"Unlocking the Power of Big Data: Insights from Global Leaders"** highlights the significant impact of big data analytics on business outcomes. The report found that:

- 85% of respondents believe that big data is critical to their business success.

- Companies that are effective at using big data achieve a 5-6% increase in productivity and 10% increase in profits.

- Big data analytics can help businesses reduce costs by 10% and improve customer satisfaction by 15%.

The report also identifies several key factors for successful big data implementation:

- **Executive commitment and leadership support:** Senior management needs to be fully committed to big data initiatives and provide the necessary resources and support.

- **Strong data governance and security:** Proper data governance policies and security measures are essential to ensure data accuracy, privacy, and compliance with regulations.

- **Talent and skills development:** Companies need to invest in developing the skills and expertise required to manage and analyze big data.

- **Agile and iterative approach:** Big data initiatives should be implemented in an agile and iterative manner, allowing for continuous learning and improvement based on data insights.

By following these best practices, organizations can leverage the power of big data to gain a significant competitive advantage in today's dynamic business environment.

8.5. Benefits of Big Data Analytics

Big data analytics offers a multitude of benefits across various domains, impacting businesses and organizations of all sizes. Here are some key advantages:

8.5.1. Cost Reduction and Efficiency Gains

It can lead to significant cost reductions and efficiency gains in several ways:

- **Identifying operational inefficiencies:** By analyzing data on production processes, resource allocation, and energy consumption, organizations can identify areas for improvement and optimize workflows for increased efficiency. This can lead to significant cost reductions and resource savings.

- **Predictive maintenance:** Big data analysis allows companies to predict equipment failures and schedule maintenance proactively, avoiding costly downtime and disruptions.

- **Targeted marketing campaigns:** By analyzing customer behavior and preferences, businesses can design targeted marketing campaigns that are more likely to resonate with their audience. This leads to more effective marketing spending and a higher return on investment.

8.5.2. Enhancing Product Development

It empowers strategic decision-making and enhances customer experiences:

- **Understanding customer needs:** By analyzing customer feedback, social media data, and purchase history, companies can gain valuable insights into customer needs and preferences. This information can then be used to develop new products and services that address those needs and ultimately improve customer satisfaction.

- **Personalized product recommendations:** Analyzing customer data allows companies to recommend products that are relevant to individual customers' interests and preferences. This personalized approach can lead to increased sales and customer engagement.

- **Identifying market trends:** By analyzing market data and competitor activity, businesses can identify emerging trends and adjust their product offerings accordingly. This allows them to stay ahead of the competition and introduce innovative products that meet evolving customer needs.

8.5.3. Strategic Decision Making and Improved Customer Experience

Big Data Analytics empowers strategic decision-making and enhances customer experiences:

- **Data-driven decision-making:** By analyzing vast amounts of data, businesses can make informed decisions based on evidence rather than intuition. This leads to better strategic decisions and improved business outcomes.

- **Customer Journey Analysis:** Understanding the entire customer journey through data analytics helps optimize touchpoints, improving customer interactions and increasing retention rates.

- **Personalized customer experiences:** By analyzing customer data, businesses can tailor their customer service and marketing efforts to individual needs. This results in a more personalized and engaging customer experience, leading to increased loyalty and satisfaction.

- **Dynamic pricing and promotions:** Big data analytics can help businesses optimize pricing strategies and develop targeted promotions based on real-time market data and customer behavior. This allows them to maximize revenue and profitability while providing value to customers.

8.5.4. Risk Management and Mitigation

It assists in identifying and mitigating various forms of risks:

- **Fraud detection and prevention:** By analyzing data on financial transactions and customer behavior, businesses can identify anomalies and suspicious patterns that may indicate fraudulent activity. This allows them to detect and prevent fraud before it occurs, protecting their financial assets and customer data.

- **Cybersecurity threats and vulnerabilities:** Analyzing network data and system logs can help organizations identify potential cybersecurity threats and vulnerabilities in their IT infrastructure. This proactive approach allows them to take preventive measures and mitigate risks before they can be exploited.

- **Predicting and managing risk events:** By analyzing historical data and real-time information, businesses can develop models to predict potential risks like natural disasters, supply chain disruptions, or market fluctuations. This allows them to proactively prepare and manage these events, minimizing their impact on operations and finances.

These are just some of the many benefits that big data analytics can offer. As businesses continue to invest in big data technologies and solutions, we can expect to see even greater innovation and value creation across industries.

8.6. Big Data in Various Sectors

Big data is revolutionizing various sectors by offering unparalleled insights and opportunities for data-driven decision-making. Here's a glimpse of how different sectors are leveraging big data:

8.6.1. Entertainment: Personalization in Media

- **Streaming services:** Analyzing user data allows platforms like Netflix and Spotify to personalize content recommendations, leading to increased user engagement and satisfaction.

- **Gaming:** Big data helps game developers understand player behavior and improve gameplay experiences through dynamic adjustments and targeted advertising.

- **Virtual reality:** Analyzing user data enables VR developers to tailor experiences to individual preferences and create more immersive and engaging environments.

8.6.2. Education: Curriculum Development and Improvement

- **Personalized learning:** Analyzing student data allows educators to tailor learning plans, identify areas needing improvement, and optimize teaching methods for individual needs.

- **Predicting student performance:** Big data models can predict student success and identify students at risk of falling behind, enabling educators to provide targeted support and interventions.

- **Curriculum development:** Analyzing data on student performance and engagement can inform decisions regarding curriculum content, teaching methods, and assessment strategies.

8.6.3. Health Care: Patient Monitoring and Disease Prevention

- **Precision medicine:** Analyzing patient data allows for personalized treatments and interventions tailored to individual genetic profiles and medical histories.

- **Predictive analytics:** Big data models can predict disease outbreaks and identify individuals at risk for developing specific diseases, enabling preventive measures and early intervention.

- **Remote patient monitoring:** Analyzing wearable sensor data allows doctors to monitor patients remotely and detect potential health issues early, improving patient outcomes and reducing healthcare costs.

8.6.4. Government and Public Sector Management

- **Crime prevention:** Analyzing crime data allows law enforcement agencies to identify crime hotspots and deploy resources more effectively.

- **Social service program optimization:** Analyzing data on program effectiveness allows governments to optimize resource allocation and improve service delivery for citizens.

- **Infrastructure management:** Big data analysis helps optimize traffic flow, energy consumption, and waste management in cities and communities.

8.6.5. Marketing and Banking Applications

- **Targeted advertising:** Analyzing customer data allows businesses to deliver personalized advertisements and marketing campaigns, increasing effectiveness and return on investment.

- **Fraud detection:** Big data models can detect fraudulent transactions in real-time, protecting financial institutions and customers from financial losses.

- **Credit risk assessment:** Analyzing credit data enables banks to assess creditworthiness more accurately and offer personalized loan options to customers.

These are just a few examples of how big data is transforming various sectors. As big data technologies continue to evolve, we can expect even more innovative and impactful applications across all aspects of our lives.

8.7. Types of Big Data Analytics

Big Data Analytics involves four main types: Diagnostic, Descriptive, Prescriptive, and Predictive analytics. These methods use tools for tasks like data mining, cleaning, and visualization to improve the analysis of gathered data, benefiting companies.

8.7.1. Diagnostic Analytics:

Diagnostic analytics is an advanced type used to investigate data and answer the question, "Why did it happen?" It helps understand the reasons behind behaviors and events, like identifying anomalies such as unexpected changes in product sales. Techniques include searching for patterns, filtering data, and using probability theory.

Benefits: Better understanding of data, finding answers to company questions, and comprehending customer behavior.

8.7.2. Descriptive Analytics:

Descriptive analytics is common for staying updated on trends and operational performance. It involves simple mathematical operations to analyze raw data, producing statements about samples and measurements. It's crucial for tasks in finance, production, and sales, such as creating financial reports and metrics.

Benefits: Helps companies make sense of large amounts of raw data, focusing on critical areas, and understanding the current business situation.

8.7.3. Predictive Analytics:

Predictive analytics forecasts future outcomes based on historical data, using statistical algorithms and machine learning. It helps in anticipating trends, making proactive decisions, and understanding potential future scenarios, such as predicting customer churn or forecasting sales.

Benefits: Anticipating future trends, proactive decision-making, and optimizing strategies based on data-driven insights.

8.7.4. Prescriptive Analytics:

Prescriptive analytics builds on descriptive and predictive analyses, suggesting solutions for optimizing business practices through simulations. It recommends the best steps forward based on data insights. **For example,** Google used prescriptive analytics in designing self-driving cars, where real-time data helps the cars make decisions.

Benefits: Optimizing business practices, making informed decisions, and guiding companies on the best steps forward.

8.8. Big Data Analytical Tools and Technologies

8.8.1. Hadoop and Spark Frameworks

- **Hadoop:** An open-source framework for distributed storage and processing of large datasets. It uses a distributed file system (HDFS) and MapReduce programming model.

- **Spark:** A fast and general-purpose cluster-computing framework that provides in-memory data processing for large-scale data processing and analytics.

- **MapReduce:** A programming model for processing and generating large datasets that Hadoop uses.

8.8.2. Data Integration Software

Data integration tools help combine and unify data from various sources. Examples include:

- **Apache Nifi:** A powerful data integration tool for moving and transforming data between systems.

- **Informatica PowerCenter:** A widely used ETL (Extract, Transform, Load) tool for data integration and transformation.

- **Microsoft SSIS (SQL Server Integration Services):** An ETL tool for building data integration and workflow solutions.

8.8.3. Stream Analytics Tools

Tools for real-time data processing and analytics on streaming data:

- **Apache Flink:** A stream processing framework for big data processing and analytics.

- **Apache Kafka:** A distributed streaming platform that enables the building of real-time data pipelines.

8.8.4. Distributed Storage Solutions

Storage solutions designed for handling large-scale and distributed data:

- **Amazon S3 (Simple Storage Service):** A scalable object storage service in the cloud.

- **HBase:** A distributed, scalable, and NoSQL database built on top of Hadoop.

- **Apache HDFS:** Distributed file system designed for storing massive datasets across clusters of machines.

- **Apache Cassandra:** A highly scalable and distributed NoSQL database designed to handle large amounts of data across multiple commodity servers without a single point of failure.

8.8.5. Predictive Analytics Hardware and Software

Tools and technologies for predictive analytics and machine learning:

- **TensorFlow and PyTorch:** Open-source machine learning frameworks.

- **IBM SPSS Modeler:** Software for predictive data analytics and machine learning.

- **Graphics processing units (GPUs):** Massively parallel processors designed for accelerating machine learning algorithms.

8.8.6. Data Mining Tools and NoSQL Databases

Tools for extracting insights and patterns from large datasets:

- **RapidMiner:** An open-source platform for data science, machine learning, and predictive analytics.

- **MongoDB:** A NoSQL database for storing and retrieving data in a flexible, JSON-like format.

8.8.7. Data Warehouses

Data warehousing solutions for storing and managing large volumes of structured data:

- **Amazon Redshift:** A fully managed data warehouse service in the cloud.

- **Snowflake:** A cloud-based data warehousing platform with features for data sharing and analytics.

These tools and technologies play crucial roles in handling the volume, variety, and velocity of big data, enabling organizations to extract valuable insights and make data-driven decisions.

CHAPTER 9

SYSTEM SECURITY

CHAPTER 9:

SYSTEM SECURITY

In the realm of scalable system design, the importance of robust system security cannot be overstated. As systems expand in size and complexity, they become more vulnerable to a variety of security threats, making the need for comprehensive security measures more critical than ever. This chapter aims to provide an in-depth understanding of system security, its challenges, and the strategies to mitigate risks effectively.

System security is a fundamental aspect of designing scalable systems. It involves protecting systems from unauthorized access, damage, or theft, and ensuring the confidentiality, integrity, and availability of data. As systems grow, they often become targets for various security breaches, which can have devastating impacts on business operations and user trust. Therefore, implementing robust security measures is not just a necessity but a priority in system architecture.

We will begin by understanding the various types of system security violations and their significance. The chapter will cover core principles and terminology essential for grasping the complexities of system security. We will also discuss the current challenges in the field, including the evolving nature of threats and the increasing sophistication of attackers.

We will explore breaches of confidentiality, integrity, availability, theft of service, and Denial of Service (DoS) attacks. The chapter will also examine program threats like viruses, Trojan horses, spyware, logic bombs, and worms, providing insights into their impact and mitigation strategies.

Further, we will focus on system threats, including worm attacks in networks, port scanning, and various types of Denial-of-Service attacks. Identifying these threats and understanding their prevention mechanisms is crucial for maintaining system security.

The chapter will then guide you through various security measures for system protection, covering aspects like physical security, human security, operating system security, and networking system security. These measures are vital in creating a secure environment for both hardware and software components of a system.

Finally, we will look into the challenges and solutions for system security. This includes access control, network security, data security, malware protection, incident response and recovery, compliance and audits, employee training and awareness, software and system updates, and cloud and third-party security.

9.1. Understanding System Security Violations

9.1.1. The Significance of System Security

Defining System Security

System security refers to the protection of computer systems and information from unauthorized access, use, disclosure, disruption, modification, or destruction. It encompasses a broad range of measures and technologies designed to safeguard the confidentiality, integrity, and availability of data and systems within an organization.

The evolution and growing importance in the digital era

In today's digital age, system security is more important than ever. As our reliance on technology grows, so does the potential for cyberattacks and other security threats. These threats can have a significant impact on businesses, organizations, and individuals, causing financial losses, data breaches, reputational damage, and even physical harm.

The evolving nature of technology also presents new challenges for system security. The proliferation of mobile devices, cloud computing, and the internet of things (IoT) has expanded the attack surface and created new vulnerabilities that attackers can exploit.

Here are some key factors driving the growing importance of system security:

- **Increased reliance on technology:** Organizations and individuals are increasingly reliant on technology for everyday activities, making them more susceptible to cyberattacks.

- **Sophistication of cyberattacks:** Attackers are constantly developing new and sophisticated techniques, making it more difficult to defend against cyber threats.

- **Growing volume and value of data:** The volume and value of data stored electronically is increasing exponentially, making it a more attractive target for attackers.

- **Regulatory compliance requirements:** Many industries are subject to data privacy and security regulations, requiring organizations to implement robust security measures.

- **Public awareness and expectation:** The public is becoming increasingly aware of the risks of cybercrime and expects organizations to take appropriate security measures to protect their data.

9.1.2. Core Principles and Terminology

Fundamental Concepts: Threats, Attacks, Vulnerabilities

- **Threats:** Threats refer to potential dangers or harmful events that can exploit vulnerabilities in a system. These can be intentional, such as cyberattacks by hackers or unintentional, such as natural disasters or system failures.

- **Attacks:** Attacks are deliberate actions taken to exploit vulnerabilities and compromise the security of a system. Cyberattacks, for example, may include malware infections, denial-of-service attacks, or phishing attempts.

- **Vulnerabilities:** Vulnerabilities are weaknesses or flaws in a system's design, implementation, or operation that can be exploited by threats to compromise the system's security. These can be in the form of software bugs, misconfigurations, or gaps in security protocols.

Introduction to the CIA Triad: Confidentiality, Integrity, Availability

- **Confidentiality:** Ensures that information is accessible only to those authorized to access it. It involves protecting sensitive data from unauthorized access or disclosure.

- **Integrity:** Focuses on maintaining the accuracy and reliability of data. It ensures that data is not tampered with or altered by unauthorized entities.

- **Availability:** Ensures that information and resources are available and accessible when needed. It involves preventing disruptions and ensuring timely access to services.

9.1.3. Current Challenges in System Security

The rise of modern cyber threats poses substantial risks to both organizations and individuals. From sophisticated malware to identity theft, these challenges demand a comprehensive understanding of their nuances and the subsequent impacts on security landscapes.

Overview of Modern Cyber Threats and Security Breaches

- **Modern Cyber Threats:** Malware, phishing, denial-of-service attacks, advanced persistent threats, and insider risks threaten the integrity of digital ecosystems.

- **Security Breaches:** Data breaches, identity theft, ransomware attacks, and supply chain vulnerabilities underscore the pervasive nature of contemporary security challenges.

The Impact on Organizations and Personal Data

- **Impact on Organizations:** Financial losses, operational disruptions, reputational damage, and regulatory consequences are repercussions organizations face in the wake of security incidents.

- **Impact on Personal Data:** Privacy violations, identity theft, emotional distress, and a loss of trust highlight the personal toll of security breaches, emphasizing the need for robust protective measures.

9.1.4. Common Forms of Security Breaches and Their Impacts

There are many different types of security breaches, but some of the most common include:

- **Data breaches:** These occur when confidential or sensitive data is accessed, disclosed, or stolen without authorization. Data breaches can have a significant impact on individuals and organizations, leading to identity theft, financial loss, and reputational damage.

- **Malware attacks:** These involve the use of malicious software, such as viruses, worms, and Trojan horses, to gain unauthorized access to a system or network. Malware can cause a variety of problems, including data loss, system crashes, and identity theft.

- **Denial-of-service (DoS) attacks:** These attacks attempt to overwhelm a system or network with traffic, making it unavailable to legitimate users. DoS attacks can disrupt operations and cause significant financial losses.

- **Phishing attacks:** These attacks involve tricking users into revealing sensitive information, such as passwords or credit card numbers, by posing as a legitimate entity. Phishing attacks can lead to identity theft, financial loss, and data breaches.

Impact of security breaches:

Security breaches can have a wide range of negative impacts on individuals and organizations, including:

- **Financial losses:** Businesses can lose money due to data theft, fraud, and business disruption. Individuals can lose money due to identity theft, credit card fraud, and other financial crimes.

- **Loss of reputation:** Organizations can suffer damage to their reputation if they experience a security breach. This can lead to lost customers, partners, and investors.

- **Legal ramifications:** Organizations can be fined or sued if they fail to comply with data privacy and security regulations.

- **Psychological harm:** Individuals can experience emotional distress, anxiety, and depression as a result of identity theft and other cybercrimes.

9.2. Types of Security Breaches

Delving into security breaches is essential for grasping diverse threats. From compromising data confidentiality to disrupting services, these breaches can jeopardize the pillars of confidentiality, integrity, and availability.

9.2.1. Breach of Confidentiality

This occurs when unauthorized individuals gain access to sensitive information that should be kept private. This can include personal data, financial records, intellectual property, and confidential communications. Common methods used to achieve this include:

- **Phishing:** Fraudulent emails or websites designed to trick victims into revealing personal information.

- **Social engineering:** Exploiting human trust and psychology to gain access to sensitive information.

- **Hacking:** Targeting vulnerabilities in computer systems and networks to gain unauthorized access.

9.2.2. Breach of Integrity

This occurs when unauthorized individuals modify data without permission, potentially leading to incorrect information and compromised systems. This can include:

- **Data manipulation:** Tampering with data to alter its meaning or value.

- **Malware injection:** Embedding malicious code into systems to corrupt data.

- **Man-in-the-middle attacks:** Intercepting and modifying communication channels.

9.2.3. Breach of Availability

This occurs when authorized users are prevented from accessing data or resources they need. This can be achieved through:

- **Denial-of-service attacks:** Overwhelming systems with requests to prevent legitimate users from accessing resources.

- **Ransomware attacks:** Encrypting data and demanding payment for its decryption.

- **Physical destruction of data or systems:** Disrupting the normal operation of systems through physical damage.

9.2.4. Theft of Service

This occurs when unauthorized individuals use resources without paying for them. This can include:

- **Illegal access to online services:** Stealing login credentials to use services without paying.

- **Downloading pirated software:** Using copyrighted software without permission.

- **Resource hijacking:** Exploiting vulnerabilities to gain access to resources for unauthorized use.

9.2.5. Denial of Service (DoS)

This is a specific type of breach that specifically focuses on making resources unavailable to legitimate users. This can be achieved through:

- **Flooding attacks:** Overwhelming systems with a large volume of requests.

- **Distributed denial-of-service (DDoS) attacks:** Launching coordinated attacks from multiple sources.

- **Zero-day attacks:** Exploiting vulnerabilities unknown to system administrators.

9.3. Program Threats: Types and Impact

Program threats, also known as **malicious software or malware,** are programs designed to harm computer systems and disrupt their normal operation. These programs can be installed unknowingly or through malicious actions, posing significant risks to data privacy, system integrity, and overall user experience. Here, we explore five common types of program threats and their impact

9.3.1. Viruses:

Viruses are self-replicating programs that attach themselves to other programs and spread throughout a system. Once activated, they can damage files, delete data, or disrupt system functions.

Characteristics:

- **Replication:** Viruses can make copies of themselves and spread to other programs or systems.

- **Payload:** Viruses typically carry malicious code that activates and performs harmful actions.

- **Trigger:** Activation can occur upon specific events, such as opening an infected file or running a program.

Impact:

- Data loss and corruption.

- System malfunction and crashes.

- Performance degradation.

- Security breaches and unauthorized access.

9.3.2. Trojan Horses:

Trojan horses are disguised as legitimate programs, appearing harmless but harboring malicious code. Once executed, they can steal data, install other malware, or disrupt system functions.

Deceptive Programs:

- **Appearance:** Disguised as useful applications, games, or updates.

- **Payload:** Contain hidden malicious code that activates upon execution.

- **Distribution:** Spread through email attachments, infected downloads, or exploit vulnerabilities.

Impact:

- Trojans can provide unauthorized access to attackers.

- They may steal sensitive information.

- Trojans can modify, delete, or corrupt data on the system.

9.3.3. Spyware and Covert Channels:

Spyware is software that secretly monitors user activity and collects information without their knowledge or consent. This information can then be transmitted to third parties for malicious purposes.

Unauthorized Information Transmission:

- **Spying:** Monitors keystrokes, web browsing history, and other user activity.

- **Data collection:** Collects personal information, including passwords, financial data, and browsing history.

- **Transmission:** Sends collected data to remote servers without user knowledge.

Impact:

- Privacy invasion and identity theft.

- Financial loss and fraud.

- Targeted advertising and spam campaigns.

- System performance degradation.

9.3.4. Logic Bombs:

Logic bombs are programs designed to trigger a malicious action when a specific condition is met. This could be a date, time, event, or user action.

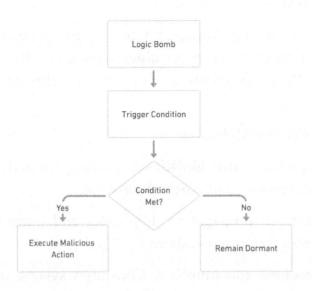

Condition-Triggered Attacks:

- **Hidden code:** Embedded within legitimate programs and activated by specific triggers.

- **Destruction:** Can delete files, format disks, or encrypt data.

- **Disruption:** Can disrupt system functions and cause crashes.

Impact:

- Unforeseen data loss and corruption.

- System failure and downtime.

- Operational disruptions and financial losses.

9.3.5. Worms:

Worms are self-replicating programs that spread rapidly across networks, exploiting vulnerabilities to infect multiple systems. They can consume resources and disrupt network functionality.

Self-Replicating Malware:

- **Exploits vulnerabilities:** Spreads through known weaknesses in unpatched software.

- **Network propagation:** Replicates and transmits itself across connected systems.

- **Resource consumption:** Consumes system resources, causing performance degradation.

Impact:

- Network congestion and outages.

- System performance degradation.

- Increased security vulnerabilities.

- Potential for data breaches and malware infections.

Understanding these different types of program threats and their impact is crucial for implementing effective security measures. By being aware of these threats and taking necessary precautions, individuals and organizations can protect themselves from the harmful consequences of malware.

9.4. System Threats: Identification and Prevention

The three major system threats: worm attacks in networks, port scanning and vulnerability identification, and denial-of-service attacks. It covers identification and prevention tactics for each threat.

9.4.1. Worm Attacks in Networks:

Worms are self-replicating programs that spread across networks, exploiting vulnerabilities in operating systems and applications. They can consume resources, steal data, and disrupt operations.

Identification: Signs of worm activity include unusual network traffic, decreased system performance, and unexplained file creation or modification.

Prevention:

- **Patching:** Regularly update operating systems, applications, and firmware to fix vulnerabilities exploited by worms.

- **Anti-malware:** Implement and keep updated anti-malware software capable of detecting and removing worms.

- **Firewalls:** Utilize firewalls to restrict unauthorized access to your network.

- **Network segmentation:** Segment your network to limit the spread of worms in case of infection.

- **User education:** Train users to recognize potential worm threats and avoid clicking suspicious links or opening unknown attachments.

9.4.2. Port Scanning and Vulnerability Identification:

Port scanning is the process of identifying open ports on a computer or network. Attackers use this information to identify potential vulnerabilities and exploit them.

Identification: Unusual network activity, especially scans originating from unknown IP addresses, could indicate port scanning.

Prevention:

- **Port filtering:** Configure firewalls to block access to unnecessary ports.

- **Vulnerability scanning:** Regularly scan your systems for vulnerabilities and patch them promptly.

- **Log monitoring:** Monitor logs for signs of port scanning attempts.

- **Use strong passwords:** Utilize strong passwords and multi-factor authentication to protect access to systems.

- **Disable unnecessary services:** Disable or uninstall services and applications that are not in use to reduce the attack surface.

9.4.3. Denial-of-Service Attacks: Types and Tactics:

Denial-of-service (**DoS**) attacks aim to overwhelm a system or network with traffic, making it unavailable to legitimate users.

Common **types** are:

- **Volume-based DoS:** Floods the target system with traffic, exceeding its capacity.

- **Protocol-based DoS:** Exploits vulnerabilities in network protocols to crash or cripple the target system.

- **Distributed DoS (DDoS):** Utilizes multiple compromised systems to launch a coordinated DoS attack.

Identification: Unusually high network traffic, slow response times, and service outages are signs of DoS attacks.

Prevention:

- **Rate limiting:** Implement rate limiting mechanisms to restrict the amount of traffic from a single source.

- **Traffic filtering:** Filter out malicious traffic using firewalls and intrusion detection/prevention systems (IDS/IPS).

- **Resource provisioning:** Ensure sufficient resources are available to handle unexpected traffic spikes.

- **DDoS mitigation services:** Consider dedicated DDoS mitigation services for critical systems.

- **Incident response plan:** Develop and test an incident response plan for effective DoS mitigation.

9.5. Security Measures for System Protection

Protecting your systems from various threats requires a multi-layered approach addressing both physical and digital aspects. Here are four key areas of focus:

9.5.1. Physical Security: Safeguarding Hardware and Facilities

Focus: Protecting physical access to hardware and facilities.

Measures:

- **Secured Entry Points:** Secure access points with locks, security cameras, and access control systems.

- **Environmental Monitoring:** Monitor temperature, humidity, and other environmental factors to prevent damage.

- **Equipment Protection:** Use tamper-proof enclosures and limited access to critical equipment.

- **Data Backup and Recovery:** Regularly back up data and have a disaster recovery plan in place.

- **Security Awareness Training:** Train employees on physical security procedures and reporting suspicious activity.

9.5.2. Human Security: Managing Access and Preventing Social Engineering

Focus: Controlling user access and mitigating social engineering attacks.

Measures:

- **Access Control:** Implement least privilege access, granting users only the permissions they need.

- **Multi-Factor Authentication (MFA):** Require multiple factors for user authentication, such as password and fingerprint.

- **Encryption:** Encrypt sensitive data at rest and in transit.

- **Security Awareness Training:** Educate employees on social engineering tactics and how to report suspicious emails, phone calls, or physical interactions.

- **Security Policies and Procedures:** Define clear security policies and procedures and enforce them consistently.

9.5.3. Operating System Security: Internal Safeguards

Focus: Securing the operating systems and applications running on your systems.

Measures:

- **Regular Updates:** Install updates for operating systems and applications promptly to patch vulnerabilities.

- **Vulnerability Management:** Regularly scan for vulnerabilities and prioritize patching based on severity and exploitability.

- **Anti-Malware Software:** Use reputable anti-malware software and keep it updated.

- **Application Hardening:** Configure applications to minimize their attack surface and disable unnecessary features.

- **Data Loss Prevention (DLP):** Implement DLP solutions to prevent sensitive data from being leaked or transferred unauthorizedly.

9.5.4. Networking System Security: Protecting Data in Transit

Focus: Protecting data travelling across your network from unauthorized access, eavesdropping, and manipulation.

Measures:

- **Firewalls:** Implement firewalls to control network traffic and block unauthorized access.

- **Virtual Private Networks (VPNs):** Use VPNs for secure remote access and data transmission.

- **Network Segmentation:** Segment your network into different zones based on security requirements.

- **Intrusion Detection and Prevention Systems (IDS/IPS):** Deploy IDS/IPS systems to detect and prevent network intrusions.

- **Data Encryption:** Encrypt all network traffic to protect against eavesdropping and data breaches.

By implementing these security measures across these four key areas, you can significantly reduce the risk of system attacks and protect your valuable data and assets.

9.6. Challenges and Solutions in APM

From malicious actors lurking in the shadows to accidental breaches, the threats are real and ever-present. But fear not, fortifying your digital fortress is within your grasp!

We will look into the essential security measures you can implement to safeguard your systems and data. We'll explore nine key areas, each brick in your impenetrable wall of defense:

9.6.1. Access Control

- **User Authentication:** Strengthen security with robust password policies and multi-factor authentication (MFA), requiring users to verify their identity through multiple means, adding an extra layer of protection.

- **Authorization:** Clearly define and assign user roles and permissions based on job responsibilities, following the principle of least privilege to restrict access only to what is necessary for each role, reducing potential vulnerabilities.

- **Account Management:** Regularly review user access rights, promptly revoking or updating permissions as roles change or upon employee departure, ensuring the access environment aligns with the current organizational structure for enhanced security.

9.6.2. Network Security

- **Firewalls:** Configure firewalls to monitor and control incoming and outgoing network traffic, establishing a barrier against unauthorized access and potential cyber threats, enhancing overall network security.

- **IDPS:** Intrusion Detection and Prevention Systems continuously monitor network activities, detect unusual patterns or behaviors, and automatically respond to potential threats, minimizing the impact of security incidents.

- **Secure VPNs:** Ensure secure remote access by using Virtual Private Networks (VPNs) with strong encryption protocols, safeguarding data transmission and protecting against unauthorized interception or access.

9.6.3. Data Security

- **Encryption:** Safeguard sensitive data by implementing encryption protocols for both data in transit and data at rest, ensuring confidentiality and preventing unauthorized access.

- **Data Backup:** Establish regular backup procedures to safeguard against data loss, regularly testing restoration processes to guarantee data integrity and a swift recovery in case of a security incident.

- **DLP:** Deploy Data Loss Prevention tools to monitor, detect, and prevent unauthorized access, sharing, or leakage of sensitive information, maintaining the integrity of critical data assets.

9.6.4. Malware Protection

- **Antivirus and Anti-malware Software:** Regularly update and maintain antivirus software to detect and remove malicious software, providing real-time protection against evolving cyber threats.

- **Regular Scans:** Conduct scheduled and ad-hoc malware scans to proactively identify and eliminate any potential threats, minimizing the risk of malware-related incidents.

- **Email Security:** Enhance email security by filtering and scanning for malicious attachments and links, educating users to recognize and report phishing attempts, reducing the likelihood of successful email-based attacks.

9.6.5. Incident Response and Recovery

- **Incident Response Plan:** Develop a comprehensive incident response plan outlining steps to be taken in the event of a security incident, ensuring a swift and organized response to mitigate potential damage.

- **Disaster Recovery Planning:** Identify critical systems and data, establishing robust disaster recovery plans to minimize downtime and ensure the organization's ability to recover swiftly from any catastrophic event.

- **Regular Drills:** Conduct regular drills and simulations to test the effectiveness of the incident response plan, identify areas for improvement, and enhance overall incident readiness.

9.6.6. Compliance and Audits

- **Legal Compliance:** Adhere to relevant laws and regulations governing data protection and cybersecurity, ensuring ongoing compliance through regular assessments and updates.

- **Security Audits:** Conduct periodic internal and external security audits to assess the effectiveness of security measures, identify vulnerabilities, and address potential weaknesses.

- **Vulnerability Assessments:** Regularly perform vulnerability assessments and penetration testing to identify and remediate potential security risks, ensuring a proactive approach to cybersecurity.

9.6.7. Employee Training and Awareness

- **Security Training:** Provide regular and comprehensive security training to employees, ensuring they are well-versed in security policies, best practices, and the importance of maintaining a security-conscious mindset.

- **Phishing Awareness:** Educate employees about the risks of phishing attacks, conduct simulated exercises to enhance awareness, and establish a culture where employees are vigilant against social engineering threats.

- **Reporting Procedures:** Establish clear and accessible procedures for reporting security incidents, encouraging a culture of transparency and quick response to potential security threats.

9.6.8. Software and System Updates

- **Patch Management:** Regularly apply security patches and updates to software and systems, prioritizing critical updates to address known vulnerabilities promptly and minimize the risk of exploitation.

- **End-of-Life Software:** Identify and replace unsupported software to eliminate potential security vulnerabilities associated with outdated or unsupported systems, ensuring the organization's software is up-to-date and secure.

- **Configuration Management:** Regularly review and update system configurations to align with current security standards, reducing the risk of misconfigurations that could lead to security vulnerabilities.

9.6.9. Cloud and Third-party Security

- **Vendor Risk Management:** Assess and manage the risks associated with third-party vendors, ensuring they adhere to security standards and protocols, and regularly reviewing their security practices.

- **Cloud Security:** Implement and maintain cloud-specific security measures provided by the service provider, regularly reviewing and updating configurations to address emerging threats in the cloud environment.

- **Secure Integration:** Ensure secure integration with third-party services and APIs by employing robust authentication mechanisms, monitoring and auditing interactions to identify and mitigate potential security risks.

CHAPTER 10

COST OPTIMISATION

CHAPTER 10:

COST OPTIMISATION

In the intricate world of scalable system design, Cost Optimisation emerges as a crucial aspect, often determining the long-term viability and success of a project. This chapter emphasizes the significance of Cost Optimisation in designing scalable systems, addressing the challenges and strategies involved in managing and reducing costs without compromising on quality and efficiency.

As systems grow and user bases expand, it's common to see operational costs rise, sometimes exponentially. This increase can significantly impact profit margins, making Cost Optimisation an essential practice. It involves more than just cutting expenses; it's about smartly managing resources, creating effective policies for data retention, and optimizing infrastructure costs. The goal is to achieve a balance where the system not only performs efficiently but also remains financially sustainable.

The chapter will explore the factors that influence software development costs, such as technical complexity, project scope, development methodology, team composition, deadlines, and infrastructure requirements. Each of these factors can significantly affect the cost of developing and maintaining a scalable system.

We will also discuss the hidden costs in software development, including maintenance, support, integration, technical debt, training, upgrades, and security. These aspects, though not always apparent at the outset, can accumulate and become significant over time.

The chapter will then guide you through various strategies to reduce software development costs effectively. These include effective planning, agile development practices, leveraging open-source software, outsourcing, automation, code reuse, and infrastructure cost optimization. We will also explore the importance of quality assurance, testing processes, and project management best practices in cost reduction.

Finally, we address the challenge of balancing cost reduction with maintaining quality and ensuring long-term success. The pitfalls of cost-cutting strategies are examined, along with ways to maintain quality and prioritize customer satisfaction while reducing expenses.

10.1. Introduction to Software Development Costs

Software development is the backbone of our modern world, powering countless applications and services we rely on daily. But building software isn't free, and accurately estimating costs is crucial for project success. We will look into the complexities of software development costs, exploring evolving trends, the importance of cost analysis, and hidden costs to consider.

10.1.1. Evolving Trends in Software Development Expenditure

The landscape of software development costs is constantly shifting. Here are some key trends to watch:

- **Rising developer rates:** As demand for skilled developers outpaces supply, their compensation continues to climb, particularly in specialized areas like AI and blockchain.

- **Shifting development models:** The rise of cloud-based development, agile methodologies, and open-source tools can lead to cost savings, but also requires factoring in new infrastructure and training expenses.

- **Globalized talent pool:** Outsourcing development to regions with lower labor costs can be tempting, but it comes with challenges like communication barriers and intellectual property concerns.

10.1.2. Importance of Cost Analysis in Software Systems

Thorough cost analysis is vital for informed decision-making throughout the software development lifecycle. It helps:

- **Define project scope and feasibility:** Accurately estimating costs ensures projects are undertaken with realistic budgets and avoids potential financial pitfalls.

- **Optimize resource allocation:** Understanding cost drivers allows for efficient allocation of development resources, maximizing value and minimizing waste.

- **Manage stakeholder expectations:** Transparent cost analysis fosters trust and realistic expectations among project stakeholders, leading to smoother project execution.

10.1.3. Understanding Hidden Costs in Modern Software Systems

Beyond the direct costs of development, several hidden costs can inflate software project budgets:

- **Technical debt:** Accumulated technical debt from shortcuts or poor design choices can lead to future maintenance and rework expenses.

- **Integration costs:** Integrating new software with existing systems can be complex and costly, requiring careful planning and testing.

- **Security vulnerabilities:** Addressing security vulnerabilities after deployment can be costly and damage reputation, making proactive security measures essential.

After understanding these evolving trends, the importance of cost analysis, and the potential for hidden costs, you can make informed decisions and navigate the complexities of software development expenditures effectively.

Remember, investing in upfront planning and cost analysis can save significant resources and ensure project success in the long run.

10.2. Factors Affecting Software Development Costs

Accurately estimating software development costs requires a nuanced understanding of several key factors. From intricate technical challenges to efficient team dynamics, each element plays a crucial role in shaping your project's financial landscape. Let's dive into these cost drivers and equip you with the tools to navigate your software development journey with confidence.

10.2.1 Technical Complexity and Requirements

- **Technical Complexity:** The intricacy of the project, including advanced functionalities, integration with other systems, and the need for specialized technologies, significantly impacts development costs. Complex requirements may necessitate more skilled developers and additional time for implementation.

- **Requirements Clarity:** Clear and well-defined requirements reduce ambiguity and prevent costly changes later in the development process. Frequent changes due to unclear requirements can lead to increased development time and costs.

- **Technology Stack:** The choice of technologies and tools also influences costs. Licensing fees, development tools, and the need for specialized skills can contribute to overall expenses.

10.2.2 Project Scope and Scale

- **Scope Changes:** Expanding the project scope during development often results in increased costs. Changes may require additional coding, testing, and potential rework, affecting both time and resources.

- **Project Scale:** Larger projects with extensive features, data handling, or user bases generally involve more development effort, testing, and project management.

Scaling up requires careful planning to manage costs effectively.

- **Customization Requirements:** The level of customization needed, whether for specific business processes or user interfaces, can impact costs. Highly customized solutions may require more development effort and testing.

10.2.3 Development Methodology and Processes

- **Development Methodology:** The chosen development methodology, such as Agile, Waterfall, or DevOps, can influence costs. Agile methodologies may accommodate changes more easily, while Waterfall emphasizes a structured approach, potentially affecting development speed and costs.

- **Quality Assurance:** Robust testing processes are essential for ensuring software reliability. An effective testing strategy, including automated testing tools and comprehensive testing plans, can contribute to higher upfront costs but reduce post-release issues.

- **Documentation:** Adequate documentation, while essential for project understanding and maintenance, can add to development costs. However, it can save time and resources in the long run by facilitating future updates and troubleshooting.

10.2.4 Team Composition and Skill Level

- **Team Expertise:** The skill level and expertise of the development team directly impact costs. Highly skilled developers may demand higher salaries, but their efficiency and ability to address challenges can contribute to cost savings in the long term.

- **Team Size:** The size of the development team also affects costs. A larger team may expedite development but can increase coordination challenges. Smaller teams may be more cost-effective but might take longer to deliver.

- **Outsourcing vs. In-House:** Deciding whether to use in-house resources or outsource development services can impact costs. While outsourcing may provide cost savings, it requires effective communication and management to mitigate potential challenges.

10.2.5 Timeframe and Deadlines

- **Project Timelines:** The duration allocated for development directly affects costs. Rushed timelines may require additional resources or overtime, potentially increasing costs. Realistic timelines allow for better resource planning and budget management.

- **Deadlines and Penalties:** Projects with strict deadlines and penalties for delays may incur higher costs due to the need for accelerated development efforts. Balancing speed with quality is crucial to avoiding additional expenses associated with rushed work.

- **Project Phases:** The distribution of development phases over time can impact costs. Front-loading development efforts may require higher initial investments, while a staggered approach allows for more balanced resource allocation.

10.2.6 Infrastructure and Tooling Requirements

- **Infrastructure Costs:** The selection and provision of infrastructure, including servers, cloud services, and hardware, can significantly impact costs. Cloud services offer flexibility but may incur usage fees based on resource consumption.

- **Tooling Expenses:** The adoption of development tools, including integrated development environments (IDEs), project management tools, and collaboration platforms, contributes to costs. Licensing fees, training, and ongoing tool maintenance should be considered.

- **Security Measures:** Implementing robust security measures, such as secure coding practices and security testing tools, adds to development costs. However, investing in security during development helps prevent costly security breaches and post-release fixes.

- **Scalability Requirements:** Planning for scalability, whether vertical (upgrading hardware resources) or horizontal (adding servers), impacts costs. Scalable infrastructure and tools ensure the software can handle growing user loads and data volumes.

- **Maintenance and Upkeep:** Regular maintenance, updates, and monitoring of infrastructure and tools are ongoing costs. This includes addressing software vulnerabilities, applying patches, and ensuring that tools remain compatible with evolving technologies.

Understanding and managing these factors is essential for accurate budgeting and successful software development projects. Regular monitoring and adjustment of resources based on project dynamics contribute to cost-effective and efficient development processes.

10.3. Hidden Costs in Software Development

Software development is often seen as a one-time expense, but the reality is that many hidden costs can arise throughout a project's lifecycle. By understanding these costs upfront, you can make more informed decisions and avoid budget overruns. Here's a breakdown of six common hidden costs in software development.

10.3.1 Maintenance and Support Costs

Ongoing maintenance represents a substantial hidden cost in software development. Continuous updates, bug fixes, and improvements are necessary to ensure the software remains reliable and aligned with evolving user needs. Additionally, providing effective customer support incurs expenses, requiring resources for addressing user queries and issues promptly. Compatibility with new operating systems and browsers may lead to unexpected maintenance costs.

10.3.2 Integration and Compatibility Expenses

The integration of third-party services or APIs can result in unanticipated costs. Changes in external systems may pose challenges that demand additional development efforts and ongoing support. Compatibility testing across various devices, browsers, and platforms involves extra testing efforts, and issues arising post-launch may require resources for resolution. Data migration from existing systems can also introduce unexpected complexities and expenses.

10.3.3 Technical Debt and Rework Costs

Technical debt, accumulated due to rushed development or deferred tasks, often results in hidden costs. Addressing technical debt in the future requires additional time and resources. The discovery of errors or inadequacies post-launch necessitates extensive rework, with associated costs for identifying, addressing, and testing these issues. Code refactoring to adapt to future changes may contribute to unexpected development expenses.

10.3.4 Training and Knowledge Transfer Expenditures

Continuous training to keep the development team updated on new technologies and best practices represents an ongoing hidden cost. Knowledge transfer between team members or to new hires involves time and resources. Neglecting this aspect can lead to inefficiencies and errors. Furthermore, the need to keep documentation up-to-date requires ongoing effort, and overlooking this task may result in increased training and support costs.

10.3.5 Upgrades and Scalability Investments

Necessitated technology upgrades to maintain compatibility and security may lead to unforeseen expenses. Scalability investments become essential as user bases grow, requiring thoughtful planning to avoid performance issues and emergency upgrades. Scaling infrastructure to accommodate increased demand may involve unexpected costs, especially if scaling requirements were initially underestimated.

10.3.6 Security and Compliance Expenses

Regular security audits and assessments may reveal vulnerabilities, necessitating immediate attention and incurring unplanned expenses. Changes in regulations or the need to adhere to new compliance standards can lead to unforeseen costs related to legal consultations, documentation updates, and system modifications. Responding to security incidents, such as data breaches, may result in additional costs, including forensic analysis, legal fees, and potential compensation.

Being cognizant of these hidden costs in software development and incorporating them into project planning is crucial. Regular reassessment and adjustment of budgets based on evolving project needs and challenges are essential for successful software development and long-term sustainability.

10.4. Strategies for Reducing Development Costs

Building impactful software often collides with budgetary constraints. This guide provides a strategic framework for navigating the financial complexities of software development, offering nine proven strategies to optimize resource allocation, leverage technology, and deliver value without compromising quality or innovation. Dive into agile practices, open-source solutions, and infrastructure optimization, and unlock a path to building software that delights both users and your bottom line.

10.4.1. Effective Planning and Requirement Gathering

- **Prevents scope creep:** Clearly defined requirements lead to a focused development process, avoiding costly changes later.

- **Reduces rework:** Misunderstood requirements often lead to rework, which is expensive and time-consuming.

- **Improves team communication:** Everyone involved is on the same page about the project goals, leading to smoother collaboration.

10.4.2. Agile Development Practices and Iterative Approaches

- **Faster feedback loops:** Frequent releases allow for early user feedback, helping to identify and address issues quickly.

- **Reduced risk of failure:** Smaller, incremental releases minimize the impact of mistakes and make it easier to adapt to changing needs.

- **Increased team morale:** Working on smaller, achievable goals keeps the team motivated and engaged.

10.4.3. Leveraging Open-Source Software and Existing Technologies

- **Reduces development time and cost:** Open-source libraries and frameworks offer pre-built functionality, saving time and resources.

- **Increases code quality:** Open-source code is often well-tested and documented, leading to more reliable software.

- **Improves interoperability:** Leveraging existing technologies ensures your software can integrate with other systems seamlessly.

10.4.4. Outsourcing or Offshoring Development

- **Access to lower talent costs:** Outsourcing to regions with lower labor costs can be a significant cost-saver.

- **Specialized expertise:** You can tap into a wider pool of talent with specific skills and experience.

- **Focus on core competencies:** Outsourcing non-essential tasks frees up your internal team to focus on core activities.

10.4.5. Automation and Continuous Integration

- **Reduces manual effort:** Automating repetitive tasks frees up developers for more strategic work.

- **Improves code quality and consistency:** Continuous integration ensures code is constantly tested and integrated, leading to fewer bugs.

- **Faster deployments:** Automated deployment processes enable faster delivery of new features and updates.

10.4.6. Code Reuse and Modularization

- **Reduces development time and effort:** Reusing existing code components saves time and avoids duplicating work.

- **Improves maintainability:** Modular code is easier to understand, update, and debug.

- **Increases flexibility:** Modular components can be easily combined to create new functionality.

10.4.7. Infrastructure Cost Optimization

- **Choose the right cloud platform:** Selecting the right cloud provider can significantly impact your infrastructure costs.

- **Optimize resource utilization:** Regularly review and adjust your cloud resources to avoid paying for unused capacity.

- **Automate infrastructure management:** Automated tools can help you manage your infrastructure efficiently and cost-effectively.

10.4.8. Quality Assurance and Testing Processes

- **Prevents costly bugs:** Thorough testing identifies and fixes bugs early, avoiding expensive rework later.

- **Improves software quality:** Higher quality software leads to happier users and fewer support costs.

- **Boosts team confidence:** Knowing the software is well-tested gives the team confidence in their work.

10.4.9. Project Management Best Practices

- **Clear communication:** Open and regular communication keeps everyone informed and aligned.

- **Effective risk management:** Proactive identification and mitigation of risks helps avoid project delays and cost overruns.

- **Continuous monitoring and reporting:** Tracking progress and performance allows for course correction and optimization.

10.5. Balancing Cost Reduction with Quality

In any business, achieving a balance between cost reduction, maintaining quality, and ensuring long-term success is crucial for sustained growth. This delicate equilibrium requires strategic planning, careful decision-making, and a focus on customer satisfaction. Let's look into key aspects of this balance:

10.5.1. The Pitfalls of Cost Reduction Strategies

While cost reduction is often necessary for improving efficiency and competitiveness, it can lead to pitfalls if not managed judiciously:

- **Shortsighted Cuts:** Slashing budgets without considering long-term consequences can lead to compromised quality, reduced innovation, and employee morale issues. Think beyond immediate savings and prioritize sustainable cost management.

- **Focus on Quantity over Value:** Sacrificing quality for mere output quantity can damage brand reputation, customer loyalty, and future sales. Remember, value creation is key, not just cost reduction.

- **Ignoring Process Improvement:** Simply cutting corners without addressing underlying inefficiencies won't yield lasting results. Invest in process optimization to eliminate waste and improve cost-effectiveness.

- **Neglecting Employee Engagement:** Cost-cutting measures that demotivate or disenfranchise employees can backfire. Foster a culture of cost-consciousness and collaboration for sustainable success.

10.5.2. Maintaining Quality While Cutting Costs

Achieving cost reduction without compromising quality requires a strategic approach:

- **Process Optimization:** Identify and streamline inefficient processes to improve productivity and reduce operational costs without sacrificing quality.

- **Supplier Negotiations:** Negotiate favorable terms with suppliers and explore alternative, cost-effective sources without compromising the quality of inputs.

- **Technology Integration:** Leverage technology to automate tasks, enhance efficiency, and reduce labor costs while maintaining or improving product or service quality.

- **Continuous Improvement:** Implement a culture of continuous improvement, encouraging employees to suggest and implement cost-saving measures without compromising quality standards.

- **Focus on Preventive Maintenance:** Proactive maintenance of equipment and infrastructure can prevent costly breakdowns and ensure product quality is consistent.

10.5.3. Prioritizing Customer Satisfaction

Customer satisfaction is paramount for long-term success, and it should remain a focal point even during cost-cutting initiatives:

- **Value Proposition:** Ensure that your product or service continues to provide value for customers, even if there are cost reductions. Communicate the value proposition effectively to maintain customer loyalty.

- **Transparent Communication:** Keep customers informed about any changes in products, services, or pricing structures. Transparency builds trust and can mitigate negative reactions to cost-cutting measures.

- **Customer Feedback:** Actively seek and respond to customer feedback. Use it as a tool for improvement, identifying areas where cost reductions may impact satisfaction and addressing concerns promptly.

- **Investing in Customer Experience:** Allocate resources to enhance customer experience, recognizing that long-term success often hinges on customer loyalty and positive word-of-mouth.

Cost Optimisation

Achieving a balance between cost reduction, quality, and long-term success requires a holistic and strategic approach. It involves optimizing processes, engaging employees, and prioritizing customer satisfaction to ensure that cost-cutting measures contribute positively to the overall health and sustainability of the business.

REFERENCE

https://auth0.com/learn/rest-vs-soap

https://www.altexsoft.com/blog/what-is-grpc/

https://www.geeksforgeeks.org/system-security/

https://globalkinetic.com/2021/02/24/the-5-pillars-of-good-solution-architecture-security/

https://www.amazon.com/Security-Computing-Charles-P-Pfleeger/dp/0134085043

https://owasp.org/

https://www.sans.org/apac/

https://www.microsoftpressstore.com/store/software-estimation-demystifying-the-black-art-9780735605350

https://www.amazon.com/Agile-Estimating-Planning-Mike-Cohn/dp/0131479415

https://www.ibm.com/blog/application-monitoring-best-practices-whats-the-best-approach-for-your-business/

https://www.dotcom-tools.com/web-performance/list-of-application-monitoring-tools-apm/

https://www.harness.io/blog/software-application-monitoring-best-practices

https://www.dotcom-monitor.com/learn/what-is-application-monitoring/

https://www.section.io/blog/scaling-horizontally-vs-vertically/

https://www.redhat.com/en/topics/cloud-native-apps/what-is-an-application-architecture

https://learn.microsoft.com/en-us/azure/architecture/guide/architecture-styles/

https://www.knowledgehut.com/blog/big-data/big-data-architecture

https://www.scaler.com/topics/design-patterns/types-of-design-pattern/

https://www.javatpoint.com/classification-of-design-pattern-in-python

https://medium.com/design-microservices-architecture-with-patterns/fundamentals-of-scalability-vertical-and-horizontal-scaling-2933422859de

https://www.ibm.com/blog/application-monitoring-best-practices-whats-the-best-approach-for-your-business/

https://www.dotcom-tools.com/web-performance/list-of-application-monitoring-tools-apm/

https://www.harness.io/blog/software-application-monitoring-best-practices

https://bau.edu/blog/big-data-analytics-types/

https://www.dotcom-monitor.com/learn/what-is-application-monitoring/

https://www.geeksforgeeks.org/system-security/

https://www.amazon.com/Security-Computing-Charles-P-Pfleeger/dp/0134085043

https://owasp.org/

https://www.sans.org/apac/

https://waydev.co/five-tips-to-reduce-software-development-costs/

https://waydev.co/five-tips-to-reduce-software-development-costs/

https://www.microsoftpressstore.com/store/software-estimation-demystifying-the-black-art-9780735605350

https://www.amazon.com/Agile-Estimating-Planning-Mike-Cohn/dp/0131479415

ABOUT AUTHORS

Huzaifa Aisf:

Huzaifa is a content creator and experienced Solution Architect with a passion for sharing his knowledge in technology. Through his tech podcasts and blogs, he explores the latest trends and insights in software architecture, drawing on his extensive experience in designing and optimizing cloud-based solutions. His background includes leading projects in fintech and various software industries. Huzaifa's goal is to combine his practical expertise with his love for teaching, helping others navigate the complex world of technology.

LinkedIn: https://www.linkedin.com/in/huzaifaasif8580/
Medium: https://medium.com/@huzaifaasif
Website: www.huzaifa.io

Asim Hafeez:

Asim Hafeez is a system design expert and technology analyst with a deep passion for educating others in his field. His expertise shines through in his well-researched articles, where he dives into the intricate world of system design, offering insights and analysis on current trends and technologies. With a rich background in system architecture and a natural flair for breaking down complex topics, Asim has made a name for himself as a knowledgeable and accessible source of information. His enthusiasm for technology is matched only by his commitment to sharing his understanding with others, guiding both novices and professionals through the ever-evolving landscape of tech.

LinkedIn: https://www.linkedin.com/in/asimhafeezz/
Medium: https://medium.com/@asimhafeez

Made in the USA
Las Vegas, NV
30 January 2024

85112299R00154